"Geraldine's book delivers what it promises! From info on first-day jitters and managing crushes to navigating menstruation, academics, and social media, readers get solid advice and learn necessary coping skills. Quotes from preteens and example scenarios normalize fears and feelings that come with middle school challenges. Activities and checklists help girls personalize and organize it all. This book will be a welcome addition to any backpack!"

—**Lisa M. Schab, LCSW**, psychotherapist; and author of twenty books, including *The Anxiety Workbook for Teens* and the teen creative journal, *Put Your Worries Here*

"*The Middle School Survival Guide for Girls* is both informative and encouraging—and a book I wish I had access to as a preteen! Geraldine does a wonderful job addressing the many different changes and pressures that young girls face during this difficult period, and provides plenty of opportunities for the young reader to build new skills, increase their confidence, and develop their sense of self-worth and self-esteem."

—**Leah Aguirre, LCSW**, psychotherapist, cofounder of Cove Counseling Group, and coauthor of *The Girl's Guide to Relationships, Sexuality, and Consent* and *Is This Really Love?*

"*The Middle School Survival Guide for Girls* is the book I wish I had when I was younger! Geraldine O'Sullivan is like the cool aunt you trust to go to for advice. She does a fantastic job using warmth and relatability to address the real concerns of incoming middle schoolers with checklists, mental exercises, and tips—all while normalizing and comforting the reader so they feel prepared. From dating to locker combinations, changing friendships and hygiene, and handling bullies and nerves, this book really covers everything that might be on your mind— and feels like a warm hug. This should be part of the mandatory reading for all rising fifth graders, I could not recommend this book enough!"

—**Sara Brenner, LCSW**, author of *A Kids Book About Therapy*

"Geraldine touches on all the key topics essential for surviving middle school emotionally, physically, and socially. Her thoughtfully designed exercises offer valuable support to every young girl navigating her place at school and in social circles. My favorite aspect is how Geraldine seamlessly integrates discussions about social pressures with practical activities, like 'positive self-talk,' to counter the negative voices so many of us hear as women."

—Sally Annjanece Stevens, LCSW, school social worker, and author of *Social Anxiety Workbook for Teens*

"As an acceptance and commitment therapy (ACT) expert and psychologist—and a parent who's navigating the middle school years—I highly recommend *The Middle School Survival Guide for Girls*. This workbook combines practical tools, like a first-day checklist, with deeper life skills such as goal setting and values exploration. It empowers girls to navigate challenges, discover their strengths, and build resilience—making it an essential guide for thriving during this pivotal stage of life."

—Diana Hill, PhD, host of the *Wise Effort* podcast, and author of *The Self-Compassion Daily Journal*

"A complete resource book written in easy-to-understand language, *The Middle School Survival Guide for Girls* is a must-read for preteen-to-adolescent girls. Geraldine O'Sullivan has created easily accessible narratives, activities, and tools to help girls navigate this often-difficult time period. From the emotions they might feel at school to engaging appropriately in social media, girls (and their parents) will embrace the social, emotional, and psychological lessons in this workbook."

—Tory Cox, EdD, LCSW, author of *The Art of Becoming Indispensable*

the MIDDLE SCHOOL SURVIVAL GUIDE FOR *Girls*

The Inside Scoop on Dealing with
School, Friends, Emotions, and
Other Big, Big Changes

GERALDINE O'SULLIVAN, LCSW

Instant Help Books
An Imprint of New Harbinger Publications, Inc.

Publisher's Note

This publication is designed to provide accurate and authoritative information in regard to the subject matter covered. It is sold with the understanding that the publisher is not engaged in rendering psychological, financial, legal, or other professional services. If expert assistance or counseling is needed, the services of a competent professional should be sought.

INSTANT HELP, the Clock Logo, and NEW HARBINGER are trademarks of New Harbinger Publications, Inc.

New Harbinger Publications is an employee-owned company.

Copyright © 2025 by Geraldine O'Sullivan
Instant Help Books
An imprint of New Harbinger Publications, Inc.
5720 Shattuck Avenue
Oakland, CA 94609
www.newharbinger.com

All Rights Reserved

Cover design by Amy Shoup

Interior design by Tom Comitta

Acquired by Georgia Kolias

Edited by Elizabeth Dougherty

Printed in the United States of America

25 24 23

10 9 8 7 6 5 4 3 2 1   First Printing

To the trusted adults who supported me
and the ones who continue to support students every day—
your compassion, patience, and dedication
are making a difference.

DISCLAIMER

This book is presented solely for educational purposes. The author and publisher are not offering it as legal, therapeutic, or other professional services. While best efforts have been used in preparing this book, the author and publisher make no representations or warranties of any kind and assume no liabilities of any kind with respect to the accuracy or completeness of the contents and specifically disclaim any implied warranties of merchantability or fitness of use for a particular purpose. Neither the author nor the publisher shall be held liable or responsible to any person or entity with respect to any loss or incidental or consequential damages caused, or alleged to have been caused, directly or indirectly, by the information or programs contained herein. No warranty may be created or extended by sales representatives or written sales materials. Every mental health professional is different, and the advice and strategies contained herein may not be suitable for your situation. This book is not designed to be a substitute for mental health or medical care, and you should seek the services of a competent professional before making significant changes or life decisions. While this book reflects common situations and experiences, the characters, entities, names, and content are purely fictional. Any likeness to actual persons, either living or dead, is strictly coincidental.

CONTENTS

FOREWORD XI

WELCOME XIII

CHAPTER 1: It's the First Day of School, Now What? 1

CHAPTER 2: Getting to Know Yourself 21

CHAPTER 3: Taking Care of Yourself 37

CHAPTER 4: School Isn't the Only Thing Changing—
Your Body Is Too 55

CHAPTER 5: Understanding Emotions, Feelings,
and Moods 71

CHAPTER 6: Forming Friendships: Knowing If It's
Fake, for Now, or for Real 87

CHAPTER 7: Crushes, Catching Feelings,
and Consent 107

CHAPTER 8: Finding the "Me" in Social Media 125

CHAPTER 9: Responding to Pressure.........................143

CHAPTER 10: Figuring Out Family...............................161

FINAL WORDS: Not Just Surviving, but Thriving...........177

REFERENCES..179

FOREWORD

As a psychologist who has specialized in the world of adolescent girls for the last 30 years and the mother of two young women, I've witnessed the growing pressure and complexities girls in middle school face. Middle school is an intense phase of human development, filled with radical transformations, intimidating new stressors, and moments of profound growth. These years are hard, which is why you rarely hear grown women fondly reminiscing about the joys of middle school. More likely, it's a stage remembered for its stabbing bouts of insecurity and relentless emotional tenderness.

The middle school years represent a unique period of physical, emotional, and social changes that can be challenging for girls and parents alike. Girls are dealing with vast physical shifts while simultaneously facing more complex social dynamics and academic pressures. As our first generation of digital natives, young girls today are also the population segment most vulnerable to the stresses that come with the digital world. Despite its significance, middle school is often overlooked as a stepping-stone between childhood and adolescence, and girls lack resources to help them navigate its unique challenges.

It's no wonder I am grateful and honored to introduce Geraldine O'Sullivan's *The Middle School Survival Guide for Girls*. From start to finish, this book serves as a wise and friendly companion for girls facing the challenges and adventures of middle school. It's a landscape O'Sullivan clearly knows well, as chapter by chapter she navigates typical challenges and scenarios with care and kindness. Her spot-on examples of middle school experiences are so relatable, girls will feel seen and soothed as they soak in her helpful information.

This guide gently takes readers by the hand and walks alongside them as they face middle school. It creates a safe space to reflect on their experience and make sense of things they don't necessarily want to bring up to their parents or peers. Readers can easily navigate the myriad of firsts that come their way—feelings, crushes, *that* time of the month, and school dances—with confidence and resilience.

To every girl who picks up this book: May these pages guide and comfort you. With each chapter and exercise, you'll feel more confident, capable, and prepared for your middle school experience.

—Lucie Hemmen, PhD
author of *The Teen Girl's Anxiety Survival Guide*

WELCOME

Welcome! If you've picked up this book, that means that you're in middle school, or you'll be starting middle school soon. Middle school is an exciting time, and it comes with lots of changes, challenges, and adventures. While some people might still see and treat you like a kid, others might be expecting you to act like an adult and take on lots of new responsibilities. It can be confusing to figure out where you fit into all of this. In middle school, you'll have so many opportunities to expand your horizons, make new friends, learn new skills, and have new experiences. Some of these opportunities will be easy and fun. Some decisions that you'll make might be more complicated and require a little more thought.

On the first day of school, you'll be learning who your new teachers are, where your new classes are, and how to open your locker. Don't worry, you'll figure all these things out with a little time and patience. Your schoolwork will start to get more challenging, and you'll be learning new study skills to help you stay organized. You'll be meeting new people. You may be joining new clubs or sports teams. Start by taking it one day at a time, and pretty soon you'll be feeling confident about your new school!

In middle school, you're at that in-between age where you're not a little kid in elementary school anymore, but you're not a fully fledged teenager either. This is a fun time to explore who you are and what you're interested in. You'll be learning to identify your values, your interests, what clothes and music you like, and who you are becoming as a young woman. This is also an important time to practice taking care of yourself—physically, mentally, and socially. Since middle school brings increased responsibilities, taking care of yourself becomes extra important! Eating, sleeping, exercising, and having healthy friendships will set you up to tackle anything that comes your way.

Physically, you'll likely be going through puberty during middle school—so you'll be getting to know your body and your emotions even better. As you read this book, you'll learn how to navigate the changes going on in your body, as well as any emotional changes you might be experiencing. You'll learn how to identify your feelings, emotions, and moods as well as how to use healthy coping skills when times get tough.

You may notice that things start to change with your friendships as well. Some friendships from elementary school will still be there, other friendships might end if they're not working for you anymore, and new friendships will form. You'll be navigating handling social media, maybe getting a phone, and setting boundaries. As you and your friends get crushes or start dating, this can affect you socially as well. But don't worry, you'll have fun experiences! And even when they're challenging, you're still going to learn a lot.

At the same time that you're learning and forming your values, you might also be pulled in different directions socially. There can be moments of social pressure. You may find yourself in situations where you're pressured to ditch class, gossip about others, vape, or do something you're not ready to do. The guidance in this book will help you to figure out how you want to handle these situations before you find yourself in them.

As you change and grow as an individual and within your friendships, you might also notice that the dynamics in your family change a bit as well. You might start to get even closer with your parents or guardians as you share what's going on in your life. Or there could be increased tension with them as your priorities change or if you don't agree with the expectations they've set for you. For some girls, their family situation might change if they move houses, their guardian gets a new job, their parents get divorced or remarried, or they experience a loss. This book will help you gain skills to navigate these types of challenges while still being successful in school.

At the end of the day, it's not just about surviving middle school—it's about *thriving*! These are fun and formative years of your life. You'll make funny, lasting memories with your friends. You'll experience a lot of exciting firsts. You'll overcome obstacles and achieve great things. And, yes, there will be awkward, embarrassing, and challenging moments too—but that's okay. You'll have the tools you need to handle those moments when they come up. Know that you're not alone, and that all girls go through similar experiences to you at this age.

So, as you start reading this book, find a cozy chair, get comfy, and grab a journal and a pen to help you complete the activities alongside this book. You've got this!

IT'S THE FIRST DAY OF SCHOOL, NOW WHAT?

"I start school tomorrow and I'm excited, but I'm nervous too. I feel like when I walk in the classroom everyone is gonna be staring at me."

—Ashlynn, age 12

In middle school, it's normal to be feeling a lot of different emotions. You might be excited about this new chapter, happy about seeing your friends again after summer, optimistic about school, and confident in yourself. It's also totally normal if you're feeling nervous about figuring out where your classes are, shy about meeting new people, afraid you'll forget your locker combination, apprehensive about homework, and self-conscious about how you look. No matter how you're feeling, know that you're not alone and that other girls are feeling the same way!

You might be wondering things like: How do I find all my classes? What will I wear? Do I have the school supplies that I need? What if I don't know anyone? Where do I get picked up after school? Try to remind yourself that everything will get figured out, and you'll get through this! There are lots of ways to prepare yourself beforehand. The more prepared you are, the better you'll feel on day one and beyond. If you are feeling nervous, this chapter will go over lots of ways to help you stay calm and stress less.

Remember that middle school is going to be fun. You'll be making new friends, learning new study skills, and gaining new independence. You'll also be learning new ways to stay organized and communicate with teachers, which will help you to feel confident in your classes. Let's take a look at how you can prepare for your first day.

PREPARING FOR YOUR FIRST DAY

In the last few days of summer, there are some things that you can do to help you prepare to start middle school. It's normal to be excited but also a little nervous about all the changes, especially if you're going to a new school. Let's take a look at Evie's experience as she prepares for her first day.

> *Evie is starting middle school next week. She's looking forward to it, but last night she dreamed that she got lost and was late to her classes. Tomorrow, she and her dad are going to go to her middle*

school so that she can learn the campus and figure out where her classes are ahead of time. She's hoping that once she actually sees the school she'll be able to figure things out more easily on the first day. She's worried that she'll be the only one who doesn't know what they're doing!

Like Evie is doing, it's a great idea to go check out a new campus with your parent or guardian before school actually starts. Some schools will provide your schedule ahead of time, which will make finding your classrooms easier. But even if you don't know your schedule yet, it can still help to go to the school to see where you'll get dropped off or get the bus. Some schools offer an orientation to help you get acclimated to everything.

Some schools send out a list of school supplies that you'll need, but not all schools do this. Before school starts, it's a good idea to get one notebook for each class, a binder with dividers, lined paper, pencils, pens, highlighters, some folders, and a planner. Have fun choosing the styles and colors that you like! School supplies can be expensive, so if it's hard for your family to buy everything that you need, try asking your school, local library, or community center if they have any free school supplies.

Most middle schools assign lockers to students, which can be a big change from elementary school. Some lockers have built-in combination locks, some schools provide you with a lock for your locker, and other schools ask you to bring your own. If you have time to learn your combination ahead of time, that's great. If you won't receive your lock until the first day, go easy on yourself and know that it might take a few tries to get it right. You can always ask your locker neighbor, a friend, or a teacher to help you figure it out if you are having trouble. You may want to write down your locker combination in more than one place, so that you don't lose it, but it's best not to share your locker combination with anyone at school.

Middle school is a fun time to figure out how you like to express yourself, and what you feel comfortable wearing. On the first day, it's a good idea to wear an outfit that you feel both confident and comfortable in. You might want to wear layers in case it's really hot outside but cold in your classroom. Pro tip: Don't forget to check your school's dress code to make sure that your outfit doesn't break any rules.

On the first day of school, it will help if you're not feeling too tired or rushed. Try to go to bed a little earlier than normal the night before. Have your backpack ready to go and your outfit planned. If you have siblings who will be trying to use the bathroom at the same time in the morning, set your alarm a little earlier to give yourself extra time to get ready. Plan enough time to eat breakfast before you leave. If you're taking the bus, make sure you know the bus route and where to get picked up. If your family is driving you, see if it's possible to leave earlier in the morning in case there's traffic at the drop-off area. There is usually more drop-off traffic the first week of school while everyone is getting used to how things work. Doing these things can be helpful so that you don't feel too rushed.

Of course, you can't plan for *everything,* but preparing a little bit ahead of time, like Evie, will help you to feel more confident and ready for your first day.

FIRST-DAY CHECKLIST

To help you have a successful first day, create a personalized checklist for what you need to do in advance and what you want to pack. Here are some ideas to get you started:

- ☐ Visit the campus and learn where the different buildings, classrooms, and bathrooms are.
- ☐ Check if my schedule is available ahead of time. Ask an adult to help.
- ☐ Browse my school website to learn what my school has to offer.
- ☐ Shop for school supplies.
- ☐ Plan my first-day outfit.
- ☐ Learn my locker combination.
- ☐ Talk to my parent/guardian about how I'll be getting to and from school.
- ☐ Figure out how long it will take me to get ready in the morning.
- ☐ Go to bed on time (or early!).
- ☐ Set my alarm (maybe even start waking up early a few days beforehand).
- ☐ Make sure the school nurse knows if I need to take any medicines at school.

Here are some ideas about what to put on your packing list to bring on the first day:

- ☐ backpack
- ☐ school supplies
- ☐ water bottle
- ☐ personal items like your wallet, phone, house key, glasses, or retainer
- ☐ personal toiletries like lip balm or menstrual supplies if you use them
- ☐ locker combination
- ☐ class schedule
- ☐ PE clothes, if applicable
- ☐ food for a snack and lunch

Know that you'll be able to handle whatever comes your way. If your day doesn't go 100 percent as planned, you can learn from those experiences and start again tomorrow!

HANDLING NERVOUSNESS

When we start something new, we may feel nervous about what to expect. Being *nervous* means feeling worried or fearful about a situation. Nervousness usually decreases once the situation has passed. People are designed to feel nervous when there is a threat or unknown experience, so that we can protect ourselves. Thousands of years ago in cavewomen days, people felt nervous around a threatening animal, dark locations, or unknown terrain. In middle school, you might feel nervous about whether people are judging you, if you'll embarrass yourself, or if your crush will notice you.

Feeling nervous is different for everyone. Some girls get clammy hands, and some girls get sick to their stomachs. Others, like Evie, might have bad dreams about things that could go wrong. Some might feel like it's hard to take a deep breath, while others might cry or breathe heavily. Some girls might not feel any of these feelings, while others might feel all of the above! If you are feeling nervous, this section will give you skills to cope with those feelings.

Let's take a look at how Adriana felt before her first day of school.

> *The night before her first day of middle school, Adriana was fully prepared. She'd showered, packed her backpack, set her alarm, laid out her clothes for the next day, and even memorized her locker combination. As she got into bed, she felt optimistic. But no matter how hard she tried, she couldn't fall asleep! She kept thinking about whether or not her friends would be in her classes,*

if she would be late, and if people would think her new haircut was cute. She tossed and turned for hours until she finally fell asleep.

Even when we do everything right and are fully prepared, we might still feel nervous about things that can happen. If you feel like this, know that it's okay and that the feeling will most likely pass once you get used to everything. Even though Adriana felt prepared and wasn't aware that she was nervous, her brain was working overtime! Sometimes feeling nervous can make it hard to fall asleep or stay asleep. Even if you're not feeling nervous about school, we all feel nervous sometimes. The following tips can help you manage those feelings if they come up.

There are many ways that you can help yourself when you start to feel nervous. For example, reassuring yourself by using *positive self-talk* can be really helpful. Positive self-talk simply means being kind in what you tell yourself. Breathing techniques, like taking slow, calming breaths, can help. There are also relaxation exercises that work for some people. Try a few suggestions from the list on the next page to see what works for you.

SIGN OF FEELING NERVOUS: TROUBLE FALLING OR STAYING ASLEEP

WHAT TO DO: Lie down in bed with your eyes closed. Practice "4-7-8" breathing. Inhale through your nose as you count to four. Hold your breath while you count to seven. Exhale through your mouth as you count to eight. Repeat until you fall asleep.

SELF-TALK: "It's okay if I can't fall asleep yet. I'll fall asleep whenever I'm ready. Breathing like this feels relaxing. Even if I'm not sleeping, this is still a good way for my body to rest."

SIGN OF FEELING NERVOUS: UPSET STOMACH

WHAT TO DO: Lie down or sit comfortably. Put one hand on your stomach and the other on your heart. Practice abdominal breathing, where you inhale through your nose until you can feel your stomach rising a bit. As you exhale through your mouth, you'll feel your stomach go down as air releases. Count in your head as you breathe. Try to exhale longer than you inhale. You can also listen to a favorite song or ask your parent/guardian if there's anything they recommend, like ginger candy or peppermint tea.

SELF-TALK: "This feeling will pass, and I'll be okay. I'm just feeling like this because my body got a little nervous. I'll feel better once I take some time to rest and distract myself."

SIGN OF FEELING NERVOUS: SWEATING AND CLAMMY HANDS

WHAT TO DO: Try the "5 senses" exercise to help you stay present and distract yourself from stressful thoughts.

- Look around and find 5 things you can see.
- Then find 4 things you can feel. Notice how each feels to touch.
- Next find 3 things you can hear. Tune in to the sounds.
- Then find 2 things you can smell.
- Last, find 1 thing you can taste.

SELF-TALK: "Wow, my hands are clammy! I must be feeling nervous. It's okay, though. I can just wipe them on my jeans and figure out a way to relax. I'll probably get over it pretty soon."

SIGN OF FEELING NERVOUS: FEELING DIZZY OR LIGHTHEADED

WHAT TO DO: Try a guided meditation. You can use an app or search for free guided meditations online. Find a comfortable seat or lie down, put in your earbuds, and try the meditation for five to ten minutes or longer. The meditation might guide you through some breathing exercises, use positive self-talk, or ask you to picture a calming place.

SELF-TALK: "There's nothing to worry about. I'll be okay. I can try to relax for a few minutes and then see how I feel. I'm probably just nervous about everything, but I'll feel better soon."

SIGN OF FEELING NERVOUS: BREATHING FAST AND HEART RACING

WHAT TO DO: Try "box" breathing.

- Picture a square in your mind.
- Breathe in through your nose for four seconds as you imagine your breath moving across one side of the square.
- Hold your breath for four seconds as you imagine moving across the next side of the square.
- Breathe out through your mouth for four seconds as you imagine moving across the next side of the square.
- Hold your breath for four more seconds as you imagine completing the square.
- Repeat several times.

SELF-TALK: "My heart is beating so fast! But I'm going to try some calming breaths. Slowing down my breathing for a few minutes should help me feel better pretty soon."

SIGN OF FEELING NERVOUS: FEELING TEARFUL

WHAT TO DO: Let it out! Sometimes we need to cry and not keep it bottled up. There's nothing to be ashamed of if you cry. If you can, find a safe space to let out those feelings, like a counselor's office or the school nurse's space. Often you will feel more relaxed once you let it out.

SELF-TALK: "It's kind of embarrassing that I'm crying right now. But it's fine. Everyone cries sometimes, and it's not a big deal. Maybe I can go to my counselor's office for a little bit until I'm ready to go back to class."

It's a good idea to try out a few of these techniques ahead of time to see what you like best and which ones work for you if you need them. Some people find that listening to music, talking to a friend, taking a walk outside, or journaling are helpful too.

For Adriana, once she finds a good way to relax and fall asleep, she'll be even more likely to have a good day at school. She probably just had a hard time sleeping the night before school because she was excited and a little nervous. If she finds herself in that same situation again, she'll know she has options for things to try that might help her.

The activity on the next page will help you explore a new way to journal about your feelings.

CLUSTER JOURNALING

Writing in a journal is a great way to process feelings. Sometimes journaling can help to get your thoughts out and on to paper, so that they don't keep floating around in your mind. With "cluster journaling," you start with one main idea in a circle in the middle of the page. Next you draw lines out from that circle and add new circles with different ideas. Here's an example:

Grab your journal and try it! Create as many bubbles as you want for all the different thoughts that come to mind. Once you've done this for five minutes, spend five more minutes writing about how you feel. Here are some ideas to get started:

- Writing all those thoughts down made me feel...
- I didn't realize that I...
- I'm planning to...so that I...
- I'm hoping that...
- I wonder if...
- Now I understand that...

As you're wrapping up, try to end on a positive note. Remind yourself of what is helpful to you. Now take a deep breath and see how you're feeling.

DEVELOPING STUDY SKILLS

In elementary school, were you the kind of girl who had everything neatly organized and easy to find? Or did your backpack look more like a random assortment of crumpled papers, sticks of gum, and a form you were supposed to get signed months ago? In middle school, academic expectations and responsibilities increase. Take a moment to think about what kind of student you'd like to be—and how you'll make that happen.

You'll have different teachers, who will have unique personalities and teaching styles. Don't expect to figure them all out on the first day. It likely will take some time to get used to the various expectations and requirements that each teacher will have. Developing new and improved study skills will help you stay on top of everything you need to do.

Let's take a look at Denise's experience below.

Denise has been in middle school for a little over a month. She likes her teachers, and Mrs. Mackenzie has high expectations. One of the rules she's pretty strict about is putting your name on your paper. If you don't, you lose ten points automatically. Denise is a good student, but she keeps forgetting to put her name on her paper. Her teacher is getting frustrated. Denise has been working hard to remember and stuck a sticky note on her planner to remind herself.

As you too learn new study skills, in general, the main themes to focus on are organization, dedication, and communication. With these principles in mind, you'll stay on the right track.

ORGANIZATION

When it comes to getting organized, consider the following questions:

- Do you have a planner? If so, do you actually use it? Using a planner each day to track your homework and other commitments is a great way to stay organized and to remember things.
- Next, think about where you'll study. Will it be a desk? Kitchen table? Couch? Lying down on the floor? Find a well-lit place where you can comfortably and consistently do your homework.
- Does your backpack have different compartments that you can put things in? Take some time to figure out the school supplies you'll need for each class and how you'll organize them in your locker and your backpack.

Staying organized will help you avoid losing things or getting overwhelmed by the different tasks in your classes.

DEDICATION

Part of how well you'll do in school depends on how dedicated you are. Being dedicated to something means making it a priority and staying committed to your goals. That may look like going to tutoring even when your friends are going to the mall. Or putting your phone away in order to focus on your math homework. It may mean starting assignments early instead of waiting until the last minute. When you get clear about your goals in school (for example, "I want to get at least a B in my language arts class"), it will be easier to commit to your goals and make them happen.

COMMUNICATION

Communication is a key part of succeeding academically in middle school. Make an effort to participate in class. Let your teachers know if you're struggling. Ask about tutoring or extra credit. Let your school know if you need to be absent and find out from your teachers what work you'll miss. Talk to your friends about your assignments. You can make flash cards and quiz each other before tests. Even if you're just venting about classes and homework, keeping schoolwork a part of your conversations means you're keeping it a priority.

Denise was having trouble remembering to put her name on her paper, and it was affecting her grade. But by staying organized, sticking a note on her planner to remind herself, staying dedicated, and communicating with her teacher, she'll be back on track in no time.

GOAL-SETTING

Each year of middle school is a brand-new start! You'll have new teachers and chances to expand your skill sets. Grab your journal and let's get clear on your goals and how to achieve them. Here are some examples:

GOAL: I want to improve in math this year.

STEPS I CAN TAKE: Let my teacher know about my goal. Write the assignments in my planner. Go to tutoring. Ask a friend for help.

GOAL: Get my homework done and remember to turn it in!

STEPS I CAN TAKE: Create a routine for when and where I do my homework each day. Try not to procrastinate. Take breaks when needed. Turn it in at the start of class!

Now, write down your own goals. Choose as many goals as you'd like and list steps you can take to move closer to meeting them.

Taking the time to consider the goals you'd like to achieve in middle school and the steps you can take to achieve them will help to increase your confidence. Remember that you've got this! You've planned, prepared, reflected, and developed some good coping skills for managing any stressful feelings that may come up. Don't forget to have fun!

GETTING TO KNOW YOURSELF

"I love singing; I would sing all day long if I could. I've done different choirs and stuff since I was like seven. My mom says I'm pretty good. I heard that the choir director at my new middle school is kind of intense though and that there's way more practices. So hopefully it'll be okay."

—Emma, age 12

When faced with all the exciting opportunities and changes of middle school, it's a good idea to spend some time getting to know yourself and learning who you are *right here, right now*. By understanding who you are and what is important to you, you'll be better able to tackle complicated decisions and make choices in middle school that feel true to who you are. One way to do this is to identify and explore your values, strengths, and sources of self-esteem.

What's most important to you in life? Those things are your *values*. So far, you likely learned what to value from your parents, culture, caregivers, teachers, and other people you are raised with. For example, some parents value education, and make sure their kids study hard and get good grades. Some parents value family, and teach their kids that family always comes first. Other parents value religion, and take their kids to a temple, church, or place of worship every week. In elementary school, it's common to share the same values as your parents or caregivers. As you get older, you may start to think about these values and also about your own values—and if they are the same or different. Values guide you and help you make decisions for yourself, according to what is most important to you. You also might meet friends or classmates who were raised with different values from yours, and that's okay too.

Strengths are the things that you are good at or positive qualities you have. For example, you might realize "I'm good at softball" or "My friends say I'm a good listener" or "I am determined." Those things are all strengths! Strengths take time to develop, and you'll keep gaining more as you get older. Some strengths come naturally, and others you have to work hard at developing. Don't worry if you aren't sure what you're good at yet—middle school is going to give you lots of opportunities to find out!

Self-esteem is how you feel about yourself. When you understand your values and strengths, you build the self-esteem that helps you handle difficult decisions and situations. When you have high self-esteem, you feel good about yourself. When you have low self-esteem, you feel bad about yourself and maybe put yourself down. Self-esteem is a work in progress. Some days, you will feel really good about yourself. Other days, you will feel awful.

With the many changes and new experiences of middle school, as well as developmental changes in your body, your self-esteem will likely change from time to time. That's okay! The goal is to stay kind to yourself, appreciate your strengths, and create healthy self-esteem over time so you feel confident and make healthy decisions for yourself.

 ## YOUR VALUES

Some values stay the same your whole life, and other values change as you get older. This is a normal part of growing up. The way you prioritize values, or consider them in order of importance, might change too. Your values might be different from other people's values, and that's okay. It's important to respect other people's values even if they're different from yours. Let's look at how Mariko's values started changing in middle school.

> *Every Friday, for as long as Mariko can remember, her family has gathered for movie night. Her mom makes popcorn, and she sits with her sisters to watch together. When Mariko started middle school, she made new friends who ask her to hang out on Fridays. So far, she's said no. But this week, they are going to a movie she really wants to see. Mariko values her family, and she has fun at her family movie nights. But she wants to hang out with her friends more too. It never felt this hard to choose before!*

What Mariko is going through is common. She feels like she must choose who is more important to her. At home with family, she'll have a good time. She would also have a good time with friends. She worries that if she doesn't go with her friends, she'll miss out, and on Monday, when they're talking about how much fun they had, she will feel left out. There's no right answer for what Mariko should do. It's up to her to decide what is best for her. It could be a good idea for Mariko to talk to a parent about how she's feeling.

Your parents or guardians might understand better than you think. At this age, you might care more about what your friends think than you used to. You might want to talk to them more, and you might want to hang out with them more too. That's normal! Values shift and change. There might be times when you prioritize family and enjoy quality time with them. Other times, you might choose to hang out with friends instead. Your value of education might even take priority as you complete homework instead of spending time with anyone! So let's explore your values with this next activity.

VALUES

Grab a journal or notebook and complete the following sentences. Choose which value each girl is honoring when she's making certain decisions. Then check your answers below.

1. AJ's neighbor asked them to come over after school yesterday, but AJ has a big project due tomorrow that they haven't finished. AJ really wants to hang out, but they stay home to work on the project instead because they are prioritizing the value of _____.

2. Christina's friend said she figured out how to cheat on an upcoming math test. She offered to show Christina the answers but Christina said no. This is because Christina values _____.

3. Maria's best friend, Cecile, is having a birthday party. Maria spent a long time picking out a gift and wrote a really nice card. Maria really values her _____ with Cecile.

4. Adhira's parents are from India, and she has been taking classical Indian dance classes. She really enjoys dancing and will perform in a show soon. She goes to the classes and practices because she values her _____.

5. Emily has a crush on Jason, and he offered her a hit from his vape pen. She doesn't want to make things awkward, but she said no because she values her _____.

6. Nikki's little brother wanted her to play video games with him. Nikki was busy messaging her friend and didn't really feel like hanging out with her brother. But when he asked again, she gave in and said yes because she prioritized her value of _____.

ANSWERS: More than one value could go with each of these scenarios. Here are some possible answers:

1. education, commitment
2. honesty, education, hard work
3. friendship, relationship
4. culture, family
5. health, relationship with her parents
6. family

Now, make a list of your own values. Write down as many things that are important to you as you can think of. Then think about the ways you honor them at different times and in different ways in your life.

YOUR STRENGTHS

Everyone has strengths, whether they realize it or not. It's not realistic to be good at *everything*, but all of us have positive qualities and things we're good at. Remember, you don't have to be the best at something in order for it to be a strength. For example, you can be good at soccer without having to be the captain.

Why is it important to think about your strengths? Knowing what your strengths are can help you make decisions about how you spend your time, choose which activities you get involved in, and help you feel good about yourself. In middle school, you might compare yourself to others, wondering if you're as smart or as funny as someone else. Sometimes when we compare ourselves to others, we focus on things we don't have or things we think might be negative qualities. Instead, it's much more helpful to think about your strengths and all the positive qualities that you *do* have! Let's look at Imani's experience.

> *Imani is in seventh grade. At the end of the year, Ms. Martinez gave out awards to everyone in language arts class. Melanie got "Best Listener," Brian got "Funniest," Olivia got "Most Likely to Be President," and Jackson got "Best Spelling." Imani kept thinking,* Which one am I going to get? Am I good at anything? *Finally, Imani was given her award, "Most Patient." Surprised, Imani thought about her award.* I guess I am patient, *she realized.*

Imani had never before thought in any detail about what she is good at or what positive qualities she has. Sometimes, we're aware of our own strengths. Other times, it is helpful for someone else to point them out to us. If you have a hard time coming up with your strengths, think about what your parents, grandparents, teachers, or friends compliment you for. You can also ask yourself, *What do my friends like about me? Why are they friends with me?* That might help give you some insight.

What if you just don't feel like you have that many strengths or haven't figured out what they are yet? Middle school is a great time to branch out and try new things to figure out what you might be good at. There are so many new clubs and sports to try. Just because you've never played basketball before doesn't mean you can't start now! You might not realize how helpful you are until you try volunteering somewhere. You could be really good at video editing, but you won't know unless you join the film club! Sometimes your interest in something is a clue that you might be good at it. Remember, it can take time and practice to develop strengths. It may not happen overnight. Imani learned that everyone in her class has their own unique strengths, and no one's strength is better or more important than someone else's—everyone is unique! Let's do an activity to find your strengths.

FINDING YOUR STRENGTHS

Take a look at these sentences. Then, in a journal, fill in the blanks with your strengths. Here's an example from the first question.

EXAMPLE: The last time I felt really proud of myself was when I ran the mile in PE faster than I did last year. I guess this means that one of my strengths is being athletic. (You could also write running, perseverance, commitment, or another strength here.)

1. The last time I felt really proud of myself was when I _____.
   I guess this means that one of my strengths is _____.

2. I had a hard time last year when _____.
   I overcame that challenge because I _____.
   So, one of my strengths must be _____.

3. My friend _____ likes being friends with me because I am _____.
   So that must be one of my strengths too.

4. The kindest family member I have is _____.
   When they say nice things to me, they say I'm _____.

5. The last time I helped someone with something was when I _____.

This must mean I'm _____.

So far, you've probably identified at least five strengths. In your journal, make a list of any other strengths you can think of. Here's a short list of strengths to help get you started.

EXAMPLES OF POSITIVE QUALITIES: kind, patient, athletic, intelligent, hardworking, helpful, considerate, funny, honest, fair, strong, resilient, trustworthy, creative, organized, and more!

EXAMPLES OF THINGS YOU MIGHT BE GOOD AT: reading, writing, art, sports, helping around the house, video games, listening to friends, leadership, playing an instrument, solving problems, helping someone when they're sad, being a team player, following the rules, being on time, gardening, and more!

YOUR SELF-ESTEEM

Self-esteem is how you feel about yourself. When you have low self-esteem, you feel negatively about yourself. You may struggle with confidence, have negative thoughts about yourself, and may not want to participate in activities. When you have high self-esteem, you feel positively about yourself. You might feel more confident about your capabilities and be more willing to branch out and try new things. No one feels amazing about themselves all of the time, but building healthy self-esteem is important, partly because it can affect your mood. If you feel good about yourself, you'll feel happier in general. It can also affect decisions you make about who you hang out with and what you do in your free time.

There are lots of things that can affect your self-esteem. Things that can boost your self-esteem include receiving compliments, accomplishing a task, winning a game, getting a good grade, overcoming a challenge, or helping someone. Things that can harm your self-esteem include mean comments, focusing on the negative, and comparing yourself to others on social media. Let's take a look at Carissa's experience on a day when she was struggling with her self-esteem.

> *Carissa spent time creating and posting a reel to her social media account. She carefully paid attention to all the details—the angles, the filters, and the background. She felt satisfied when she posted it and then the likes started popping up. One by one, her friends and people she didn't even know were liking and commenting on her post! She felt great until suddenly, she got a comment that*

said, "This is dumb" then later another that said, "You're ugly."
Suddenly, Carissa felt terrible. She started questioning herself
and wondering if the comments were true. She looked back at her
post and thought, Ugh, I do look ugly. *She ended up feeling*
bad the rest of the day.

Carissa's self-esteem was affected when she read reactions to her social media posts. *Bullying* is when someone intentionally says something or does something to hurt someone else. Mean online comments, like "You're ugly," is called *cyberbullying* (more on this later in chapter 6), and it made Carissa feel bad about herself.

When you experience low self-esteem, it affects the way you think about yourself and talk to yourself. Have you ever caught yourself thinking things like *I'm so stupid* or *I'll never get it right* or *I can't do this* or *She's way prettier than me?* Those types of thoughts are a form of what's called *negative self-talk* and can be a sign that your self-esteem needs support!

In middle school, it's normal to want to fit in and have friends. You might even be paying extra close attention to what others in your class say or worry about what they think about you. Sometimes all the social pressures can make it hard to keep up healthy self-esteem. But don't worry! There are things you can do regularly to help build up your self-esteem, so you don't have as many low moments.

Earlier in the chapter, you got to know your values and strengths. If you start to feel down about yourself, remember all the great qualities that make you,

you. Here are some ideas for things you can do when you are feeling down to remember how great you are!

- Refer back to the list of strengths to remind yourself how awesome you are.
- Think of one thing each day that you're grateful for. If you have a bad day or feel bad about yourself, it's easy to focus on negative thoughts or things that went wrong. Thinking of one thing you're grateful for can help you keep a healthy perspective.
- Try a kindness challenge, where you do something kind or helpful each day for one month. You'll be amazed how good it will make you feel about yourself when you've been kind and helpful to others. If you want, keep it up longer than a month!
- Make time for activities that you enjoy. If you love writing poetry or riding your bike, try to do it as often as you can and enjoy how you feel during the activity.

So, what can Carissa do to help her feel better? When it comes to her self-esteem, she could practice talking to herself in a kinder, more helpful way. Instead of saying to herself, *Ugh, I do look ugly*, she could say, *I like my post and so do my friends. That person is mean, and I know I'm not ugly*. It can be hard to ignore mean things people say. Practicing positive self-talk can make it easier. Here's an activity that can help.

SELF-TALK

When you have high self-esteem, the things you say to yourself or think to yourself are usually kind. But when you have low self-esteem, you might have negative thoughts. For example, let's say that you got a bad grade on a math test that you studied hard for. If you have low self-esteem, you might think, *I'm so stupid, how could I have messed up so badly? I'm never going to pass this class.* On the other hand, if you have high self-esteem, you might think, *I'm disappointed, but I know that I can study hard and maybe ask my teacher for extra help before the next test. It'll be okay.*

You can learn to challenge negative self-talk and make it more positive in three steps:

1. **IDENTIFY NEGATIVE SELF-TALK:** Marisa didn't like my post on social media. I bet she thinks I look bad in this outfit.

2. **CHALLENGE THE BELIEF:** How do I know that that's true? Is there any evidence to make me think that Marisa doesn't like my outfit?

3. **CREATE POSITIVE SELF-TALK:** Marisa hasn't liked my post on social media yet. Maybe she hasn't seen it, or she's busy.

Here's another example of the three steps in action.

1. **IDENTIFY NEGATIVE SELF-TALK:** I'm way too tall. I'm the tallest in my grade, and everyone stares at me. I look like a freak.

2. **CHALLENGE THE BELIEF:** Is everyone actually staring at me? How do I know that for sure? Maybe they're just looking around.

3. **CREATE POSITIVE SELF-TALK:** Kids my age are growing a lot right now. Sometimes girls are taller than boys. I guess it's normal, and maybe I'm just growing faster than the others. At least I can reach high stuff in my closet.

When you catch yourself having negative self-talk, try to notice the thoughts. Once you're aware of how you're talking to yourself, ask yourself if you're being too hard on yourself. Check in with yourself to see if there's any real evidence to back up those thoughts. Would you talk like that to a close friend? It might feel weird at first, but pretty soon you'll be used to talking to yourself in a more helpful way! Let's look at one more example.

1. Identify negative self-talk: *Why bother even auditioning for the play? I know I'll never get the part I want. Jess will probably get the lead. She always gets everything she wants.*

2. Challenge the beliefs: *Wow! Would I say this to a friend if she were thinking of auditioning? I'm being pretty harsh! Am I comparing myself to others in a helpful way?*

3. Create positive self-talk: *I'll never know if I get the part if I don't try out. I like acting, and it could be fun either way. Jess has a lot going for her, but that doesn't mean that I don't have a chance.*

As you're getting to know yourself in middle school, you'll be given lots of chances to try new things and branch out. When you have a good understanding of your values and strengths, you're better able to keep building your self-esteem. It's normal for your values to change and grow, for more strengths to develop, and for your self-esteem to fluctuate. Don't be afraid to break out of your comfort zone, branch out, and try new things. These are opportunities to keep figuring out who you are and what you're good at! You never know when you'll find something new that you enjoy.

TAKING CARE OF YOURSELF

"I love taking a bath with a cleansing face mask on and listening to my favorite music."

—Crystal, age 13

You're at an age now when you're gaining independence, and your parents or guardians may be letting you make more choices for yourself. They're not choosing your outfit, reading you a bedtime story, or scheduling playdates like they did when you were a little kid. Of course, your parents are still loving and taking care of you, but it looks a little different nowadays. At this age, it might look more like cooking dinner for you, giving you rides, making sure you have what you need for school, and asking how your day was. Now that you're getting older, it's important to develop healthy habits to take care of *yourself*—physically, personally, and mentally.

One of the best ways to help you succeed academically is to make sure that you're taking care of yourself physically. This means getting enough sleep, eating nutritious meals and snacks, taking care of your hygiene, and exercising regularly. When you do these things, you're less likely to get sick, and you'll have more energy to get you through the school day. When you're rested, you're better able to focus in class and retain information.

You'll be meeting new people and making new friends in addition to the ones you already have. Sometimes you'll want to spend time with friends or family, and sometimes you'll want time to yourself. Taking care of yourself personally and socially involves making decisions around how you spend your time and who you spend it with. Are you balancing out the stress of school with activities you enjoy? Are you having fun? Are you prioritizing your time in ways that align with your values? By taking care of yourself in these ways, you'll feel more balanced and able to tackle the responsibilities of school.

Throughout middle school, there might be times that you find yourself struggling mentally or emotionally. You or someone you know might deal with challenges like family problems, grief or loss, mental health symptoms, pressure to use drugs, or problems with friendships or relationships. Part of taking care of yourself mentally involves building a support system of people you can count on. If you know who your trusted adults are, including at school and at home, it can be easier to work through these challenges and to remember that you don't have to do it alone!

TAKING CARE OF YOUR PHYSICAL HEALTH

Let's take a moment to think about your daily habits and choices. Are you the type of girl who stays up too late on her phone or the type of girl who goes to bed early? When you want a snack, do you reach for an apple or Flamin' Hot Cheetos? Do you spend hours watching TV on the couch, or do you go outside to play soccer? Making healthy choices is an important part of taking care of yourself.

Let's look at how Ciara's choices impact her physical health.

> *When Ciara started middle school, at first she didn't join any clubs or sports because she wanted to get adjusted to everything and focus on her schoolwork. But halfway through the year, she decided to join the girls' basketball team. She was nervous for the tryouts, but she made the team. During the first few days of practice, she was so tired, and her muscles were so sore! But as she continued to practice, pretty soon she was improving her skills, flying down the court, and making friends on the team. She was even sleeping better at night too.*

At first, exercising wasn't really part of Ciara's normal routine. But the more she played basketball, the better she felt!

Taking care of yourself physically includes exercise, hygiene, sleep, and nutrition.

EXERCISE: Building regular exercise into your routine whether through PE class, after-school activities, or joining a sport is a great way to take care of your health. Exercise will help your body get stronger and sleep better. It can also help boost your mood and reduce stress. Like Ciara, you can think about the types of exercise you might enjoy and find ways to build that into your schedule.

HYGIENE: Hygiene is important for your physical health too. After exercising, you'll be needing a shower! Brushing your teeth twice a day, flossing, wearing clean clothes, filing your nails, showering, and washing your hair regularly are all ways that you can take care of your hygiene and feel good too. You can make this fun and personal by choosing soap, deodorant, and skincare and hair products that you like.

SLEEP: It's important to try to get enough sleep, so that you have enough energy to get through the school day. It can be hard to go to sleep when the group chat is blowing up with messages from friends, but you need around nine or ten hours of sleep each night! Getting enough sleep helps you to stay focused and calm. It also helps keep your immune system strong, so that you don't catch colds as easily.

NUTRITION: When it comes to nutrition, try to make healthy choices for yourself. Make sure that you are eating enough, not skipping meals, and having snacks when you're hungry. Try to eat mostly healthy food. We get lots of vitamins and nutrients from healthy food, like fruits and vegetables, and this gives us the energy we need to get through the day and stay healthy. Eating good food is like putting gas in a car—we need to eat good food to fuel us throughout the day! Eating regularly is something that is healthy for us and should be enjoyable, but some girls struggle with body image and unhealthy dieting. If you or someone you know is struggling with eating issues, talk to a trusted adult for help.

In the activity on the next page, you'll create your own self-care plan!

PHYSICAL SELF-CARE

Grab a journal and answer the following reflection questions about how you include exercise, hygiene, sleep, and nutrition into daily life. Note things that you're already doing to take care of yourself and any healthy habits that you can add to those! Here are some example answers.

EXERCISE: What are my favorite ways to exercise? Am I active every day? How does my body feel after I've exercised?

EXAMPLE: I love taking my dog to the park and running around with him. I've been teaching him tricks too. I have PE every day, so I guess I'm pretty active. After I exercise, I feel tired and sweaty, and I'm also usually in a pretty good mood.

HYGIENE: What's my morning hygiene routine? What do I do during the day? At night?

EXAMPLE: Every morning, I wash my face, put on sunscreen, and brush my hair after I get dressed. I brush my teeth after breakfast. I keep wipes in my backpack in case I get sweaty during the day. At night, I take a shower, wash my hair, and brush and floss my teeth. I used to take a shower in the morning, but it was just too hectic to get out the door on time.

SLEEP: What's my nighttime routine? Am I sleeping enough? How do I feel when I've slept a lot compared to when I haven't?

EXAMPLE: I like taking showers at night and then getting into bed with my book and my favorite Squishmallow. I usually fall asleep pretty quickly. If I don't sleep enough it's *super* hard to wake up in the morning, and I usually end up arguing with my mom when she tries to make me get up.

NUTRITION: What are my favorite foods to eat? Do I like the food in the cafeteria, or do I prefer to bring food from home? Am I mostly eating healthy food?

EXAMPLE: My favorite food is pizza. My dad usually orders it for us on weekends. The food in the cafeteria is okay, but I don't like waiting in line. Sometimes I skip breakfast if I'm in a rush, so I should probably give myself more time in the morning. Overall, I think I'm eating pretty healthy most of the time.

✶ YOUR PERSONAL AND ✶
SOCIAL WELL-BEING

Taking care of yourself personally and socially means thinking about how you're spending your time and who you're spending it with. Are you an *extrovert*, a person who gets energy from spending time with friends? Or are you more of an *introvert*, a person who prefers spending time on her own? Are you spending your time in ways that align with your values (see chapter 2), or are you making some choices that you regret later? And, importantly, are you handling your responsibilities while also having fun? When you spend your time in ways that bring you joy, while also taking care of the things that you need to get done, you'll feel more balanced and ready to tackle any new challenges.

In middle school, you'll have to choose between different commitments at times. You might have less time to spend with siblings as your homework increases. Your friendships might change as your values change. You might have to skip a movie with friends to stay home with your family or vice versa. You might miss an hour of sleep because you're up late on the phone, helping a friend. Making decisions around how you spend your time is a normal part of getting older and gaining independence.

Let's take a look at how Shawna is spending her time.

Shawna is in eighth grade. Recently, she's been arguing a lot with her mom over how much time she's spending with her friends and how much time she's on her phone. She's tired of arguing all the time. This is her best year of middle school yet, and she wants to enjoy it! She has good friends, and they love hanging out at the mall and making videos for TikTok. She thinks, So what if my math grade is a little low? I can always bring my grade up later, right?

Shawna is having a hard time balancing her school commitments with her friendships. On the one hand, she's having a great time with her friends. They go to the mall and laugh for hours on the phone, sending memes and messages back and forth. But on the other hand, it's causing arguments with her mom over her math grade, and she's tired of fighting with her mom all the time.

As you become more independent, you'll get to make more decisions about how you spend your time. Like Shawna, it can be hard sometimes to balance everything. Sometimes you just want to have fun and not have other people telling you what to do! But sometimes, we need people like our parents or teachers to hold us accountable to get things done. For Shawna, she might need to create some healthy boundaries with her friends while still having fun. If she can bring her math grade up, she won't be arguing so much with her mom.

In addition to handling your responsibilities, it's also important to make sure that you're getting time to rest, relax, and have fun. Middle school comes with increased academic responsibilities, including more homework. Be sure to take breaks when you need to. Getting good at managing your time takes practice, but try to balance school, family, and friendships with time to yourself as well!

The activity on the following page can help you see how you can prioritize your different responsibilities and still have fun.

PRIORITIES

As we talked about earlier, priorities are the things that are important to you. Sometimes, you will have to prioritize one thing over another thing if you don't have enough time for both. For example, if you have a big test at the end of the week, you might prioritize studying over hanging out with friends, even though both things are important to you.

Grab a journal and create three columns. Label the first column "Things I have to do each day." Label the second column "Things I get to do each day." And label the third column "Things I want to do more." In each column, make a list. See the example below for ideas.

Things I have to do each day:	Things I get to do each day:	Things I want to do more:
make my bed, get dressed, brush and floss teeth, go to school, do my homework, do my chores, clean up after dinner, shower	have lunch with my friends, go to volleyball practice, go on my phone, read a book, pet my cat	have movie nights with friends, join a new club, hang out with my little sister

As you fill in the columns, reflect on how you're spending your time and if there are any changes you'd like to make.

There's not always enough time in the day to accomplish everything that we'd like to do. And sometimes, we have to prioritize different things that are important. But when you make time to take care of yourself personally and socially, you'll be better able to balance your commitments and have fun too!

TAKING CARE OF YOUR MENTAL HEALTH

When you take care of yourself physically and you spend your time in ways that benefit you, that will help you to stay mentally healthy too. Our emotions tend to be more balanced when the rest of our body is well taken care of. That said, there may be times when you or someone you know might struggle with mental health, and it's important to think about who you can count on in case you need any advice.

Think back to elementary school. Who were the people and what were the places at school that made you feel safe and supported? Who was nice to you? Did you have a favorite teacher? Did you have a best friend? Did you have a favorite place, like under a shady tree or in a teacher's classroom that smelled like vanilla?

There are people at school whose role is to support you and guide you along the way. Your teachers will be the ones seeing you every day and getting to know you. Since your middle school will probably have more students than your elementary school, it will take your teachers longer to get to know everyone. You may have to be proactive and let them know if you're struggling. By getting to know the adults at your new school, you'll be building your support system and making positive connections.

You might have a counselor to help you academically and personally. Some schools have a social worker, who can help you with any personal, family, or money problems. Your school might have a school nurse you can go to if you feel sick or if you get your period at school. Some schools have school psychologists to help students with learning disabilities. There also might be a coach, club moderator, security guard, or bus driver you can talk to if you need anything.

In middle school, you may be taught more information about mental health, including how to identify signs of depression, anxiety, self-harm, or eating disorders. Some red flags include things like excessive worrying, difficulty managing anger, pervasive sadness, loss of interest in normal activities, or changes in sleep or appetite. You'll likely also learn about suicide prevention, and how to get help for yourself or a friend. There may be times when you ask an adult to help you with a small challenge, like a disagreement with a friend. But there may be times where you need help from an adult for a bigger issue, like your parents' divorce, a loss, a breakup, or a safety issue. If you're ever concerned about your mental health or a friend's, it's important to talk to a trusted adult for help.

Let's take a look at Carmen's experience when she met her counselor for the first time.

Carmen started middle school last month. Everything was going fine until last week when a rumor started that Carmen had been talking to a guy her friend Grace liked. Since Carmen liked one of his pictures on social media, everyone was assuming that she was trying to get with him, and Grace was super mad at her. At lunch, Carmen couldn't take it anymore and started crying. She couldn't remember her counselor's name, but she found her office and asked if she could talk. Mrs. Jensen turned out to be super nice. She helped Carmen and Grace move past the misunderstanding.

When you talk to a counselor at school, most things will be kept *confidential*. This means that your counselor will keep it private and won't tell anyone else without your permission. However, there are three main things that your counselor would need to tell someone about, especially if they relate to your safety. Those things are:

1. Someone is hurting you or putting you in an unsafe situation.

2. You are having thoughts about hurting yourself.

3. You are having thoughts about hurting someone else.

Depending on which state you live in, there might be different laws about what types of things can be kept private. For example, things like substance use or sexual health might not be confidential depending on which state you live in. If you aren't sure what the rules are with your counselor, it's a good idea to ask before you talk about something you don't want shared.

When it comes to building your support system, don't expect to do it all in one day. It will take a bit of time to get to know your classmates and adults on campus. You can start by learning what services your school has to offer.

Now that Carmen knows who her counselor is and where her office is, she can go back again if she needs to. Since the problem has been solved, Carmen might not even need to see her counselor again! But at least she knows where she can find her if she does.

SUPPORT SYSTEM

Grab a journal and write the title "My support system" at the top of a page. You might already have some people you've identified as part of your support system. These could be friends, family members, or other trusted adults. Write down their names and positive qualities that they have.

EXAMPLE:

- My aunt. I feel like I can tell her stuff, and she doesn't judge me.
- My best friend, Kaylie. She's always had my back.
- My dog. He sleeps on my bed every night.

Now write your own list. Include as many people as you can who currently support you.

PRO TIP: Reach out and thank them for supporting you!

Next, come up with a list of people who can support you in middle school. You might not know all the answers, but write down this list in your journal and fill it in as you start learning who everyone is at school. Then you can look back at this list if you ever need it.

EXAMPLE:

- My teachers' names
- My counselor's name
- A friend I can talk to
- A family member I can talk to
- If I had a problem, the person I would talk to
- My favorite place at school where I can relax

Now that you've identified your support system, keep it handy if you ever need it. If you've struggled to identify people to write down, that's okay too. It can take time to build a list of people, and it's a process for you to get to know people. Even if you just have one or two people on your list at first, that's a great start!

By taking care of yourself, you're setting yourself up for success. Little by little, you'll find the ways that work for you to take care of yourself physically, personally, socially, and mentally. If it gets tough, know that you have adults in your corner who are there to support you!

SCHOOL ISN'T THE ONLY THING CHANGING— YOUR BODY IS TOO

"Yesterday I started my period at school. I got blood on my pants, which was embarrassing, but the school nurse was really nice. She gave me a pad and called my mom, who brought me a change of clothes."

—Jamie, age 13

In middle school, you'll navigate lots of changes that come with starting a new school: new friends, classes, activities, and responsibilities. This is a really exciting time. But school isn't the only thing changing. There are changes going on in your body too. Some girls may have noticed changes starting during elementary school, and other girls notice these changes in middle school. These physical changes are part of puberty.

Puberty is when your body is becoming more mature. Learning about puberty may seem awkward, but it doesn't have to be! Your childhood body is becoming more adult. As your hormones change, they create changes in your appearance as well. *Hormones* are chemicals that send messages to different parts of your body (like cells and organs) to control what they do. They can affect your growth, mood, and development. In early puberty, you'll notice that your breasts are developing, you may be growing taller, and you'll grow underarm and pubic hair. As you continue through puberty, you may notice body odor, acne (pimples), or mood changes. In later stages of puberty, you will start your period (*menstruation*), and your breasts and body hair become more fully developed. Your hips and thighs likely will become fuller too.

All of these changes are a normal part of growing up. Most middle schoolers will go through these changes just like you, although everybody's pace is different. You might have a friend who got her period in fifth grade and another friend who doesn't get hers until high school. Try not to compare yourself to others and trust that your body is developing in its own way on its own timeline.

If this sounds overwhelming to you, don't worry—you're not alone! Puberty is something that everyone experiences, and it means that your body is developing normally. This chapter will provide guidance on how to handle these kinds of changes, and it's a good idea to identify a trusted adult who you can talk to. Think about who you can go to if you have any questions. Some girls feel more comfortable talking to their mom, aunt, or sister. You could also talk to a counselor or healthcare provider, such as your pediatrician. If your school has a health education program that covers puberty, the teacher may answer questions you don't want to ask in class one-on-one or through a question box.

YOUR CHANGING BODY

The changes in your body during puberty are healthy and just part of the process. However, they can take some time to get used to. You may feel awkward while changing clothes in front of other people, for example. Let's consider Jenae's experience when changing in the locker room.

> *Recently, Jenae has noticed changes in her body. Her pants have been feeling tight because her hips have been getting bigger. She recently started shaving her legs and underarms and wearing a bra. When changing in the locker room for PE, she feels really self-conscious and like everyone is looking at her. She doesn't even want to change for PE, but her teacher says she has to.*

In middle school, it's a common requirement for students to change into gym clothes for PE class. You might wonder: *Why can't I just do PE in my regular clothes?* During puberty, your sweat glands change. You might notice that you sweat more than you used to and that your body has an odor when you sweat. If all students did PE in their regular clothes and then wore those clothes for the rest of the day, the classroom could get stinky very quickly! That means that students have to change into gym clothes.

As you get used to changing in a locker room, there are some tips that might make things more comfortable. If you feel sweaty after PE, keep wipes and a travel-sized deodorant in your backpack to help you freshen up. It's also a good idea to wash your gym clothes after you wear them. If you can, keep a clean spare set in your locker. Make sure you have shoes that you can exercise in, so that you don't get stuck trying to run in flip-flops!

It's common to feel a bit self-conscious at times in the locker room but you shouldn't ever feel unsafe. If anyone ever bullies or harasses you, tell a trusted adult.

Changing in the locker room has been making Jenae uncomfortable. Other girls in Jenae's class are probably feeling the same way. At this age, there's a lot of variation in people's development. Some girls may be shaving, wearing bras, and getting their period, and others may not. There's a good chance the other girls in the locker room are more focused on their own bodies than on Jenae's.

If Jenae is very uncomfortable, and it's causing her a lot of stress that she can't overcome, she can find out if there's a more private place for her to change. There might be options for her to change in an individual bathroom stall or in the nurse's office. Jenae can always talk to a trusted adult about how she's feeling.

BODY IMAGE

Body image is the way you think and feel about your body. With a healthy body image, you feel good about your body and your appearance. With an unhealthy body image, you might have negative thoughts or put yourself down. In this activity, you'll explore how you feel about your body and its changes.

Grab a journal and answer the following questions.

- What changes am I noticing in my body?
- How did I feel about my body when I was younger? How am I feeling about it now?
- What are the things I appreciate most about my body and what it can do for me?
- What things am I looking forward to about how my body will change in the future?
- What steps can I take to keep my body healthy?

GETTING YOUR PERIOD

Getting your period, also known as *menstruating*, is something that girls experience during puberty. During puberty, your body prepares you for the possibility of having a baby one day. Each month, your hormones go through a cycle. During the month, you might notice some vaginal discharge (a clear or white-ish fluid) in your underwear. This is normal, and unless there is itching, irritation, or a strong odor, you don't need to worry about it. At the end of the cycle, you'll notice bleeding from your vagina. If you notice blood on your underwear for the first time, don't freak out! This is a normal part of your body's development.

Menstruation usually starts between the ages of 10 and 15. Some girls might get their period earlier or later than that, but the average age is around 12, when many girls are in middle school. When you have a period, you'll bleed from your vagina. It can last for a few days up to a week. Some days you may experience a "heavy" period, meaning there is more blood than on "light" days. It's common for your period to be heavier at the beginning and lighter toward the end. The blood may vary in color from light pinkish red to brownish red. The consistency might also vary from watery to thicker with clots.

Your period is controlled by hormones that determine when you'll get your period, how often, how heavy it will be, and how long it will last. While a range between 21 to 35 days is normal, most women get their period approximately every 28 days. When you're young, you might not be "regular" yet, and your period can be hard to predict. Don't worry if your period doesn't come at the exact same time each month. For girls and women who are sexually active, however, a late or missed period is a sign that they could be pregnant, and they should take a pregnancy test.

You could notice changes the week before your period as well as the week of your period. Some girls experience *premenstrual syndrome* (PMS) during the week or so before their period. Symptoms can include breast tenderness, food cravings, moodiness, acne, or bloating. During their period, some girls experience cramps, low back pain, headache, or tiredness. Some girls don't have any of these symptoms at all! If any of these symptoms are severe or causing problems for you, talk to a trusted adult about how you can get help managing them. If you're worried that your period is too painful, not regular, too heavy, or something else, check with your doctor to see what they recommend.

Let's look at Olivia's experience when she got her period for the first time.

Olivia was in her history class when she suddenly felt something in her underwear that she hadn't felt before. She asked her teacher if she could go to the bathroom, and she saw blood in her underwear. She knew it must be her period because her aunt had told her what to expect. She felt a little nervous, excited, and queasy all at the same time. She went to the school nurse, who gave her a pad, and when she got home, she told her mom what had happened.

Olivia's experience is very common. With all the changes that happen in middle school, it's a good idea to expect the unexpected—and that includes your period! Whether you've already gotten your period or not, it's a good idea to be prepared. There are many different types of products that people can use, and it might be helpful to keep a pad or tampon in your backpack in case your period starts when you're at school. You could even create a period kit that includes pads or tampons, wipes, and a spare pair of underwear. Some schools have menstrual products available in the bathrooms, and many have them available with the school nurse.

You might be wondering, *How do I know what period product to use or how to use it?* Let's look at some of the different period products in more detail. How heavy your flow is will affect how effective they are and how often you need to change them for good hygiene. It's a good idea to try different options to see what works best for you. Pro Tip: Don't flush pads or tampons down the toilet! Most bathrooms are equipped with small trash cans for this purpose.

SANITARY PAD

WHAT IT IS: An absorbent pad that sticks to your underwear. They come in different sizes, thicknesses, and lengths, depending on the heaviness of your flow. You can try different ones to see what's most comfortable.

HOW IT'S USED: You open the pad's wrapper and stick the sticky side to your underwear. Many have "wings" that wrap around the sides of your underwear for added protection. This product is very easy to use.

WHEN IT'S USED: You can use different sizes or styles depending on your flow or if you are wearing it overnight. Change a pad multiple times a day, depending on your flow.

PANTY LINER

WHAT IT IS: A very thin absorbent pad that sticks to your underwear. They come in different sizes.

HOW IT'S USED: You press the sticky side down on your underwear.

WHEN IT'S USED: Panty liners are usually used on very light days, since they are not as absorbent as pads. They can also be used as backup for a tampon. Change a panty liner multiple times a day, depending on your flow.

TAMPON

WHAT IT IS: A wad of cotton, which may come in a cardboard or plastic applicator, with a string on the end. Tampons come in different sizes and absorbencies.

HOW IT'S USED: You insert the tampon into your vagina using your finger or an applicator (which you pull out and throw away). To remove a tampon, pull the tampon out using the string. It might take a few tries before you get used to using tampons.

WHEN IT'S USED: You can use a tampon whenever you want during your period. Some girls find tampons useful if they are playing sports or swimming. Change a tampon multiple times a day, usually every few hours, depending on your flow. Important note: Do not leave a tampon in for more than eight hours.

MENSTRUAL CUP

WHAT IT IS: A reusable, flexible, silicone cup that collects period blood.

HOW IT'S USED: You insert the flexible cup into the vagina and remove it when it is full. How quickly this happens depends on your flow. The cap can be washed and reused. It might take a few tries to get used to using one.

WHEN IT'S USED: You can use a menstrual cup whenever you want during your period.

PERIOD UNDERWEAR

WHAT IT IS: Absorbent underwear that absorbs period blood without using a pad or tampon.

HOW IT'S USED: You wear period underwear like normal panties. How often you change it depends on your flow, usually multiple times a day. There may be specialized washing instructions.

WHEN IT'S USED: You can wear period underwear any time during your period.

If the options seem overwhelming, or you're not sure which product is right for you, talk to a trusted adult. They might have ideas about what product you can try. For many girls, a pad is the easiest method.

It was great that Olivia was able to go to the nurse to get a pad and talk to her mom about it when she got home. It was also nice that her aunt had already explained to her about periods, so she knew what to expect.

PERIOD TRACKING

It's a good idea to keep track of your period, so that you can get to learn your body and know when to expect your next period. (If you haven't gotten your period yet, skip this section and come back to it later once you get your period.) To track your period, you can:

USE A PERIOD-TRACKING APP: If you have a smartphone, there are lots of apps that you can use to track your period and any feelings that come along with your cycle.

USE A MONTHLY CALENDAR: You can use a paper or electronic calendar. To download a period-tracking template, go to http://www.newharbinger.com/54414.

- When you start your period, mark the day that it starts on the monthly calendar.
- Each day, make notes on your calendar or in a journal (if you have a lot to write) about how you're feeling, including any symptoms, such as discomfort.
- As you finish your period and go through the rest of the month, pay attention to how you feel, especially during the week leading up to your next period, and take notes on that too.

EXPRESSING YOURSELF

In middle school, you might be thinking about ways to express yourself through your appearance, for example, experimenting with clothes, makeup, and hairstyles. When you were a little kid, your parent bought clothes for you and picked out outfits for you to wear. But by now, you're choosing your own clothes and deciding what you feel good in.

Often, what we choose to wear and how we express ourselves depends on the situation. For example, you might wear a bathing suit at the beach, but you probably wouldn't wear one to your older sister's high school graduation! Sometimes, there are certain expectations for what we wear at different times. Your school may have a dress code that they expect you to follow, or your sports team might have a uniform that they expect you to wear. You can develop your own unique sense of style while also figuring out what makes sense for different situations.

As you experiment with what feels good to you, try to remember not to compare yourself to others in unhealthy ways. Your body is developing at its own pace. While it's normal to observe what others are wearing or how they express themselves, know that you are your own unique person with your own strengths (see chapter 2 for a reminder).

Let's consider Gabriela's experience when she compared herself to a classmate.

> *Gabriela was scrolling through social media when she saw a TikTok video from a girl in her class named Ana. In the post, Ana was wearing shorts and a crop top, with her hair in a ponytail. She was smiling and dancing. Gabriela thought,* Ugh, Ana looks so good. My mom won't even let me wear crop tops. Plus, I don't like my stomach and probably shouldn't wear one anyway. *Gabriela started feeling bad about herself and later didn't finish her dinner.*

It's normal to look at what your friends are wearing, doing, and posting on social media. But sometimes when you compare yourself to others, it can take a toll on your body image. If you're noticing that you feel bad about yourself, try to remember all the things that your body can do for you and the strengths that you identified in chapter 2.

Gabriela's self-esteem and body image were affected when she saw her classmate Ana's post. Sometimes having a negative body image can lead to unhealthy behaviors, like restricting food or overexercising. For girls who struggle with unhealthy eating or exercising behaviors, this can be dangerous, and it's important to talk to a trusted adult to get help.

When it comes to social media, remember that what you see is not reality. Because of makeup, filters, and angles, someone's appearance on social media could be totally different from what they look like in real life. Resist the urge to try to achieve an impossible standard! It can be fun to play around with your appearance both in real life and on social media, but that's what it should feel like—fun. It shouldn't feel like a pressured attempt to reach an unreachable goal. And it shouldn't make you feel bad about yourself. Hopefully, it's an expression of the true you.

What can Gabriela do to help herself feel better? If she notices the negative self-talk that she's having, she can challenge those thoughts and practice being kind to herself. If she's starting to have problems with restricting her food due to unhealthy body image, she could talk to a parent or another trusted adult for help. If she's not able to stop comparing herself to others on social media in an unhelpful way, she might want to consider taking a break from her social media.

SELF-EXPRESSION JOURNALING

Grab your journal and answer the following questions.

- What is my personal style? What clothes do I like to wear and how do they make me feel?

- Do my choices on how I express myself depend on where I am? For example, is it different at school versus other places?

- As my body changes, is there anything that helps me feel better and more comfortable with its new size and shape?

- How do I express myself in photos and videos on social media?

- Do I compare myself to others? Is it helpful or healthy?

When you're making decisions about what you wear, how you act, and what you post online, think about whether those choices *feel* good, not just *look* good. Ultimately, how you feel about yourself is what's most important!

UNDERSTANDING EMOTIONS, FEELINGS, AND MOODS

"Ugh! I'm SO mad right now. I worked really hard on my homework, but Mrs. Stephens gave me a zero 'cuz I forgot to put my name on my paper. I don't know why I even try in her class if she's just gonna be like that."

—Jaqueline, age 13

If someone asked you, "How are you feeling?" you'd probably know how to answer that question. Maybe you'd say, "I feel stressed because I have a test later," or "I feel embarrassed because my teacher called on me in front of the whole class, and I didn't know the answer." But if someone asked you, "What's an emotion, and where do you feel it in your body?" you might wonder what they're talking about. Now that you're in middle school, a lot of things are changing, including your school, friends, and even your body as it goes through puberty. Though you might feel overwhelmed sometimes, it will be easier to cope with difficult situations and make healthy choices if you are able to identify your different emotions, feelings, and moods. By paying attention to the sensations in your body and the way that you feel, you'll be better able to stay emotionally balanced and make healthy decisions.

EMOTIONS: *Emotions* are sensations that you feel physically in your body. Sometimes people think emotions and feelings are the same, but they're different! Emotions are a result of chemicals working in your body. When your body goes through any experience, it releases chemicals, and then those chemicals create physical sensations. For example, imagine that you have a test after lunch that you didn't study for and, when the bell rings, your heart starts racing because you know the test is coming up. That heart-racing is actually an emotional bodily sensation.

FEELINGS: *Feelings* are what come after the emotions. Our mind recognizes the emotional sensation in the body, and then gives it a label of a feeling. So, if you notice that your heart is racing because you're not prepared for a test, you might label that feeling as "nervous." But not every emotion leads to the same feeling! For example, if you're scared of roller coasters and your heart is pounding as you wait in line to ride one, that feeling might be "fear" for you. But if your best friend loves roller coasters, and her heart is racing before she gets on the ride, that feeling might be "excitement" for her. So, even though the emotional sensation is the same in the body, the feelings label might be different in the mind.

MOODS: An emotion may create a feeling that lasts for a few minutes or a few hours, and a bunch of feelings over a period of time might create a mood. *Moods* are a state of being that are influenced by our emotions and our feelings, but they might last for hours or days or even weeks. Moods are less specific than emotions or feelings, and they're not usually caused by a single experience. For example, maybe you got a bad grade on a test, then later in the week you had an argument with a friend, and then you got grounded for talking back to your mom. You've been feeling frustrated and sad and irritable all week and then your mom says, "Why have you been in such a bad mood?" The mood is the state of being you've been in as a result of all those emotions and feelings. Middle school is a time when most people have more changes in mood because of all the physical and emotional changes they are going through, and that is totally normal.

PAYING ATTENTION TO YOUR BODY

Some people are very in touch with the sensations that they experience in their body. For other people, they're harder to notice. When you are able to notice the emotional sensations and signals that your body sends you, you can check in with yourself. This helps you stay balanced. Let's look at the emotional experiences that Sarah had on her first day of middle school.

> *Sarah had been looking forward to starting middle school. Her mom had taken her clothes shopping, and she was excited to show off a new outfit on the first day of school. But she was also freaked out about learning a new campus and meeting new people, and she wasn't sure if she knew where her classes were. The night before her first day, she set her alarm to make sure she would wake up on time and not be rushed. But in the morning, she woke up even before her alarm went off, and she felt like she was going to throw up! She couldn't figure out why she was nauseous...did she eat something weird last night? She's not sure what's going on and is wondering if she'll have to call in sick on her very first day!*

As Sarah's body is experiencing the change of starting middle school, there's a chemical reaction that creates emotional sensations in her body. When we aren't aware of our emotions or what they might mean, this can be confusing.

When you start to notice emotional bodily sensations, slow down and take a minute to explore them. Try to think about what your body might be telling you. Keep an open mind, and don't worry if you don't have all the answers right away. This takes practice and patience!

What can Sarah do to help herself through this? First, she can stay in bed and take a few minutes to notice what she's experiencing. Second, she can put a hand on her stomach, take a deep breath, and think about what these bodily sensations might mean about how she's feeling. Is she excited and really didn't want to be late on her first day and maybe that's why she woke up early? Is she feeling nervous about finding her first class and maybe that's why her stomach is in knots?

If Sarah is able to name the feeling, this will help her to be more balanced and at ease. Once you recognize the emotional signals your body sends you and are able to identify what they mean, it can help you to handle whatever you're going through! You can make more thoughtful decisions about the steps you can take to handle what you're experiencing.

The activity on the next page can help you learn about emotions and where you notice them in your body.

EMOTIONAL EXPERIENCES IN THE BODY

For this activity, grab a piece of paper and some colored pencils. Draw a picture of yourself (it doesn't have to look perfect!). Consider the scenarios below and draw arrows pointing to the parts of the body that might be affected. Then use colors and patterns to represent the bodily sensation you might feel there. There are no right or wrong answers. Everyone's body is different!

EXAMPLE: Sarah was feeling nervous about her first day of middle school. She might draw an arrow pointing to her stomach and draw squiggly lines in her stomach to show nausea.

SCENARIOS:

1. You're leaving your neighborhood coffee shop with your favorite pink drink in hand. Next thing you know, you trip and fall and spill the drink all over yourself—right in front of your crush!

2. You just found out that you got the lead role in the school play—you worked so hard for this!

3. Your younger brother just said the *meanest* thing to you.

4. Your pet just died.

5. You're at the top of the roller coaster, and it's about to drop.

6. Your teacher just called on you to read aloud in front of the whole class.

POSSIBLE ANSWERS:

1. Red arrow pointing to your cheeks, which you color bright red to show embarrassment.

2. Pink line pointing to your mouth, where you draw a huge smile because you are happy.

3. Red line pointing to your chest, where you draw squiggly lines because you are upset.

4. Blue line pointing to your eyes, where you draw tears because you are sad.

5. Green line pointing to your stomach, where you draw stars because you are excited and scared.

6. Purple line pointing to your heart, which you draw really big to show you can feel it racing because you are nervous.

FIGURING OUT FEELINGS

Okay, so, first come the emotions with those sensations in the body, and then the feelings come next, right? Right. Feelings come when we are aware of our emotional experiences and can name them. Our feelings also come from what we *think* about our emotional experiences. Like how roller coasters might feel scary for one person, but exciting for another person. Let's take a look at what happened when Estefania felt embarrassed at school.

Estefania was walking with her tray of food at lunch, when she tripped and fell. In front of EVERYBODY. The tray clattered to the ground and made a huge noise. Everyone turned around to look at her. On top of that, she was wearing a skirt, and she's not sure if anyone saw her underwear when she fell. A bunch of kids started laughing. One girl came up and asked her if she was okay. Estefania felt her cheeks turn hot and super red, she felt really sweaty all of a sudden, and her throat tightened, as though she was about to cry. She tried to play it cool and held it together as she picked up her food and the tray and put them at the drop-off window. Then she hurried out of the lunchroom and burst into tears. She didn't want anyone to see her crying, so she ran over to her counselor's office. Her counselor, Mrs. Sanchez, said, "What happened? How are you feeling?" Estefania said, "I can't go back to class after this, Mrs. Sanchez, I'm SO embarrassed."

For Estefania, it was pretty easy for her to identify her feelings here. First, her body went through the experience of falling down. Next, she experienced the physical emotional sensations of her cheeks turning red, body sweating, throat tightening, and crying. Estefania knew what this combination of sensations meant since she's felt it before: embarrassment! So, it was pretty easy for her to tell her counselor how she was feeling. Maybe, if she had tripped while alone in her room, she might have felt something else—like indifference, frustration, or silliness. But since it happened in front of everyone and some kids laughed, she felt really embarrassed.

One thing that's super important to know is that *all* feelings are okay. Don't judge yourself for any of your feelings. Sometimes people think certain feelings like anger, embarrassment, sadness, guilt, or jealousy are bad or negative. But the truth is, feelings are a normal and natural part of being a human! When we acknowledge, recognize, and name our feelings without judgment, we can work through them more easily. If we try to squash our feelings down or ignore them, we're not allowing our body and mind to go through what it needs to go through.

What if you just don't have time to work through all of those feelings? What if you have to get to class and give a presentation, and you just don't have time to cry for half an hour? Sometimes, busy schedules and social situations don't allow us to feel all our feelings in the moment. Some people like to journal at night before bed or vent by talking about their feelings to a friend on the phone later. Even if you can't feel all of your feelings in the moment, try to tell yourself that your feelings are okay and that you can check in with yourself later.

Estefania's counselor helped her by listening to her, giving her a private place to cry, and helping her feel calmer before returning to class. While she will still remember the embarrassing moment, she had the chance to work through the hard feelings. This will help make it easier for her to move on with her day and put the situation in the past. And there's a good chance everyone else already forgot about it!

The activity on the next page will help you help learn how to identify feelings.

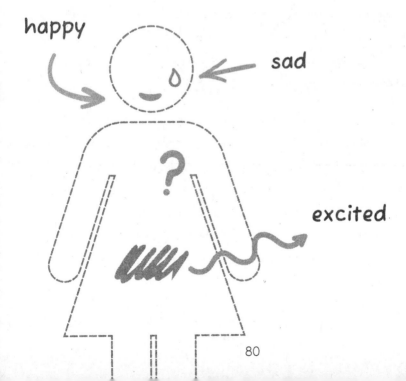

IDENTIFYING FEELINGS

In this chapter's first activity, you practiced paying attention to your body and noticing where you experience emotions in the body. Next, let's learn how to assign feelings to those emotional experiences. For example, if your best friend just moved to a different school, and you feel your throat tightening and your eyes welling up with tears, you might label that feeling "sad." Let's look at the scenarios below and see if you can think of a feeling that goes along with each experience.

SCENARIOS:

1. Jessica got in a big fight with her mom over whether or not she can go see a movie today with her friend. Her mom said no, and Jessica starts feeling hot, her face is red, and she starts yelling. She's feeling _____.

2. Sammie just got her test back from her teacher and found out that she failed. She studied so hard for it! She really thought she would do better than that. She hunches over her desk and looks down. She's feeling _____.

3. Andrea's class is going to a water park for a field trip tomorrow. Andrea *loves* water parks, and she's a good swimmer. She can't wait to see her friends tomorrow for the trip. She's feeling _____.

4. Michelle's grandma is coming to visit. She hasn't seen her grandma in a year, and she's missed her so much! She's been waiting all week for her grandma to arrive, and when she does, her grandma gives her a huge warm hug. Michelle's got a big smile on her face. She's feeling _____.

5. Justine got caught vaping in the school bathroom. The security guard just brought her down to the main office, and she's waiting to talk to the principal. The principal already called her dad, and he's on his way to the school. She's sitting in the office, tears forming in her eyes, looking down at her shoes. She's feeling _____.

There are no exact right answers to these scenarios. There are lots of words to describe feelings!

POSSIBLE ANSWERS:

1. Angry, mad, disappointed, frustrated
2. Disappointed, embarrassed, frustrated, ashamed
3. Excited, happy
4. Joyful, loved, cared for, special
5. Ashamed, disappointed, embarrassed, scared, nervous

MOODS

Moods are different from emotions and feelings. While emotions and feelings can arise quickly and can change quickly, moods last longer. Also, it's easier to figure out what caused an emotion or feeling. However, there can be lots of experiences or ongoing feelings that can form a mood. When people say that someone is in a "good mood," they usually mean that that person seems happy, optimistic, joyful, or excited. When people say that someone is in a "bad mood," it usually means that they seem angry, frustrated, sad, or sullen. Like feelings, it's okay if you are experiencing different moods from time to time! It's not realistic to expect yourself to be in a good mood *all* the time. When you're in a good mood, you can notice it, feel grateful for it, and continue on with your day. When you're in a bad mood, you can notice it, consider what might be causing it, and practice taking care of yourself. Let's look at Nuria's experience when she was going through a rough time.

Things haven't been easy for Nuria recently. Middle school is harder than she thought it would be, and her grades have been low. She always used to be good at math, but now it seems so hard. Plus, her best friend, Tanya, went to a different middle school, and she really misses her. She's making some friends, but they just don't get her like Tanya did. It seems like her little brother is more annoying than ever. Her crush at school barely notices her. With everything going on, Nuria has been really irritable recently. Sometimes she snaps at her mom for no reason. Then she feels guilty afterward. Her aunt lives with her and recently she said,

> *"Nuria sweetheart, what's going on? It seems like you've been in a bad mood for weeks!"*

Nuria's been in a bad mood because of all the hard things she's dealing with right now. What can Nuria do? Since her aunt noticed how Nuria is in a bad mood, she could open up to her aunt about what's going on. Sometimes, talking or venting to someone you trust can help you to work through the ongoing feelings that are affecting your mood. Also, Nuria may want to think about the things that are going *well* for her too. Practicing gratitude for the good things in life is a good way to boost your mood. Taking care of herself and treating her body right can also help. If she's doing all those things and continues to feel down, she could talk to an adult to help her.

Lots of things can affect your mood: experiences, weather, food, sleep, and your brain chemistry! For some people, a sunny day after days of rain can brighten their mood. Sometimes, if you don't get enough sleep, especially for several days in a row, it can cause a low mood. Sometimes, things outside of your control affect your moods. As you get to know yourself and your moods, you can use tools to support your emotional state of mind.

Hormones can also affect your mood. Have you ever heard of a "mood swing"? When people talk about *mood swings*, they mean that someone's mood changes suddenly, or maybe even for no reason. When you're going through puberty in middle school, your brain and your body are continuing to develop at a fast pace. All these changes can also come with mood swings. Also, some girls experience mood swings before their period starts. As mentioned earlier, this is called PMS (premenstrual syndrome). If you're going through this—don't worry. Just know that mood swings can be part of your development.

Remember, no one can be in a good mood all of the time. However, if you feel like you're in a bad mood all the time or if you can't even remember when the last time was that you felt like you were in a good mood, that's a good reason to talk to a parent or trusted adult about what's going on. Also, if your mood swings are so drastic that they're causing problems with your friends and family, that is another reason to ask for help. For some people, ongoing low moods or intense mood swings can be a sign of depression or another mental health issue, which treatment could help. Talk to a trusted adult about how you're feeling if you're concerned about your mood.

Did you know that there are things that you can do to help your body's moods? One great way to boost your mood is regular exercise. Exercise produces stress-releasing hormones. Getting enough sleep and eating healthy food consistently can also help balance your mood. Skipping meals can make you *hangry*, and no one wants that! Be careful with sugary or caffeinated drinks too. While they might give you a burst of energy at first, they can negatively affect your mood and make you feel really wired later.

When you're dealing with a lot of feelings, it can be very helpful to write about it in a private journal. If you are worried about someone reading it, you can tear up the pages afterward or type it in a document that you then delete. Journaling is helpful because you can be super honest about exactly what's on your mind. You can yell, scream, rage, rant, and say whatever you want on a paper and no one will judge you!

The following activity will give you a chance to practice journaling.

JOURNALING PRACTICE

For this activity, grab your favorite journal and answer the questions below. Don't worry about your handwriting, spelling, grammar, or any of that stuff. This is just for you. No one will grade it!

- How are you feeling today?
- Did you notice any sensations in your body today that caused any feelings?
- Is there anything that's bothering you or stressing you out right now?
- What's one thing that you are grateful for today?

These are just some questions to get you started, but you can write anything you want.

Whether you're writing about something embarrassing that happened at school, an argument you had with a friend, or the funny thing that happened at lunch, journaling can be an awesome way to release and work through your feelings. Being in touch with your emotions, feelings, and moods will help you cope with the changes of middle school and know if you need to reach out for help.

FORMING FRIENDSHIPS: KNOWING IF IT'S FAKE, FOR NOW, OR FOR REAL

"Monique and I have been best friends since elementary. We even have matching bracelets with our initials on them."

—Casey, age 13

Middle school is an opportunity to learn and grow both as an individual and within your friendships. Some of your friends from elementary school might be at the same middle school as you, which is a great way to continue some of those long-lasting friendships. You might be starting a new school where you don't know anyone and have to start making new friends. Or you might realize that as you're growing and changing, you've started to outgrow certain friendships and might not have the same friends that you used to have. All of these situations are normal and okay.

For some girls, making friends seems to come very naturally. They might have an outgoing, talkative personality, or maybe they're very friendly and take the time to be kind to others. For other girls, making friends feels more challenging, especially if they're shy or if they feel nervous in social situations. It doesn't matter whether you're an outgoing or shy person. It's always possible to make friends and find people to connect with! In this chapter, you'll learn skills to form friendships and how to tell if a friendship is healthy.

Some girls have lots of friends, and others might just have one or two close friends. Some girls make friends at school, community events, and through sports, and others might find it easier to make friends online through activities like playing video games or writing fan fiction. When it comes to friendships, don't forget that quality is more important than quantity—it's more satisfying to have a few closer and more *authentic* (real) friendships where you can trust one another than to have lots of friendships that are *superficial* (lacking depth or emotional attachment).

Throughout middle school, you'll notice that your friendships might shift, change, or grow over time. It's normal for there to be differences in the types of friendships that you have with people. For example, you might have a friend that you see only every once in a while because your parents are friends. Or you might have a friend that you hang out with a lot during the volleyball season because you're both on the same team, but then you don't hang out as much once the season is over. You might have a friend who makes you laugh a lot, but you don't really talk about serious stuff. Or you might have a friend you talk to every day and you feel like you can tell them really personal stuff. It's common to have different types of friendships. Some might last a long time and grow into deeper and long-lasting friendships, while others might be shorter friendships.

It's also normal for some of your friendships to end. This can happen for a variety of reasons. Sometimes, friendships end because someone moves away, and it's hard to stay in touch. Or maybe your values are changing as you're getting older, and you don't relate to a friend as much anymore. Or maybe you had a disagreement that you weren't able to recover from. Sometimes, you grow apart and friendships end naturally. Other times, you may need to end a friendship respectfully when you feel like it's not working anymore.

MAKING NEW FRIENDS

In middle school, you'll have lots of opportunities to try new activities, meet new people, and make new friends. You might be excited about all the opportunities in front of you and the people you'll meet. It's also okay if you're feeling nervous about making new friends and wondering what people will think about you. For some people, making friends is pretty easy! For others, it takes a little more patience and practice.

Let's look at how Janine was feeling on her first day of middle school.

When Janine started middle school, she didn't know anyone. All of her friends from elementary school went to a different school. Janine had never been in a situation where she didn't know anyone, and she was feeling pretty nervous. She was able to figure out where her classes were, but at lunch she felt overwhelmed. She felt like everyone knew everyone and that they were all staring at her. She thought about trying to ask a group of girls if she could sit with them, but she felt too nervous, so she sat by herself. After a few minutes, another girl came up to her and said, "Hey, can I sit with you?" Janine felt so relieved.

Like Janine, lots of girls feel shy about trying to make new friends and meet people. It's also common to feel like everyone is staring at you, even though that's probably not the case. When you start middle school, you might be in a situation where you already know people. If so, try to reach out to people who don't seem like they know anyone yet! Or, like Janine, you might be in a situation where you're feeling nervous about not knowing anyone.

Meeting people, introducing yourself, and developing a friendship with someone can take practice. If you're trying to make friends, your body language can help reflect that. For example, a person who is smiling and making eye contact is a lot more approachable than someone who is staring at their phone with their earbuds in. Standing up straight rather than hunching over, smiling at people, and making eye contact are all good ways that you can show that you're open to meeting new people.

There are also verbal ways that you can show you're interested in making friends with someone. Complimenting someone on their outfit, phone case, or shoes is a good way to start a conversation with someone. If that feels tricky, introduce yourself to someone in class by asking to borrow a pencil or what the date is and then telling them your name and asking for theirs.

It can also be helpful to put yourself in situations in which you naturally meet more people. You can definitely make friends just from being in classes together. But in addition to that, joining a club, playing a sport, or doing volunteer work are all good ways to meet more people. When you're having fun with other people your age, friendships can form naturally over time as you get to know one another and share experiences together.

The next activity covers ways to start talking to someone.

FORMING FRIENDSHIPS

Introducing yourself and making friends can sometimes feel awkward. It's not always easy to know exactly what to say. Some girls are outgoing, and it seems easy for them to make friends. For others who are shy or introverted, it can be a nerve-wracking to approach someone new. Here are some examples of how you can get the conversation started with others.

If you're outgoing and making friends feels easy for you, try the following tips for meeting new people and including girls who might be feeling left out:

- "Hi! I think we have the same math class. Want to grab lunch together after class?"

- "Ooooh! I love the stickers on your water bottle! Where did you get those? My name is Paula, by the way."

- "I'm thinking about joining the softball team. Have you ever played before?"

- "Hi! Do you want to come sit with me and my friends at lunch?"

- "Check out this meme! It's so funny. What's your @? I'll add you."

Add your own! Think of other conversation starters that feel natural for you.

If you're shy and making friends is harder for you, try the following simple conversation starters:

- "Can I borrow a pen? Thanks! I'm Kimmy, by the way."
- "When did Mrs. Coleman say this assignment is due?"
- "Hi! I was wondering if I can sit with you at lunch?"
- "What time does the bell ring?"

Add your own! Think of any simple conversation starters that can feel natural for you. Practice saying them and being mindful of your body language as well.

Don't worry if talking to new people doesn't feel natural at first. Also, don't worry if the person you're talking to doesn't respond the way that you'd hoped. Some people just don't click right away, and that's okay! Over time, you'll find people you connect with.

HAVING HEALTHY FRIENDSHIPS

When a friendship is healthy, you build each other up, feel comfortable together, have fun, and trust each other. Often, you'll have similar values as well. Signs of an unhealthy friendship include mean gossip, drama, talking behind each other's back, name-calling, and a lack of trust. However, just because a friendship is healthy doesn't mean it won't have any problems. With all friendships (and relationships in general), there will almost always be occasional disagreements. Resolving them in a healthy way is an important skill to build.

Let's take a look at how Michelle handled a disagreement with her best friend, Ana.

Michelle is starting middle school with her best friend, Ana. They've been friends for years, since elementary school. They have a really strong friendship. They often laugh together and even have the same favorite foods. Michelle was there for Ana when Ana's parents got divorced. But since starting middle school, Ana has been making a lot of new friends, and Michelle is starting to feel like Ana doesn't care about her anymore. It seems like Ana always wants to hang out with her new friends. Finally, after seeing videos on social media of Ana hanging out at a sleepover that Michelle wasn't invited to, Michelle told Ana she was hurt. Ana apologized and explained that just because she has new friends doesn't mean that Michelle isn't important to her anymore, and that she's been having a hard time trying to figure out how to balance time she spends with different friends. She promised to make more of an effort to include Michelle and focus on their friendship.

Michelle and Ana were able to communicate respectfully about this issue and work it out. In this chapter, you'll have the opportunity to learn and practice this skill.

Friendships growing, changing, and even ending is a normal part of growing up, branching out, and meeting new people. As your friendships evolve, pay attention to how your friends make you feel. Do your friends build you up? Make you feel good about yourself? Make you laugh? Make you feel heard, seen, and understood? If so, these are signs that your friendships are healthy and fulfilling. However, if a friendship makes you feel insecure, embarrassed, sad, angry, threatened, or left out, this could be a sign that the friendship is unhealthy.

In addition to forming new friendships, you'll also be figuring out new and improved ways to communicate with friends. When you have a disagreement with a friend (as Michelle did with Ana), the healthiest way to handle this is usually to talk it out respectfully in person, even though doing this can feel really uncomfortable or difficult. If talking it out in person isn't possible, you could try talking about it on the phone or texting. But remember, a lot can get misunderstood through texting, so typically in person or over the phone is best.

Sometimes, when people want to avoid the discomfort of confronting a friend, they talk to other friends about the situation or hint about it on social media instead. You might feel like it's your friend's fault for not noticing that you're upset and give your friend the silent treatment. However, those options aren't as healthy because they can cause misunderstandings, and they can make it harder to work things out in the long run.

No one is perfect when it comes to communication, and it can take time to learn how to disagree with others in a healthy way. Friendships may have disagreements sometimes, and that's okay. If you're struggling in a friendship and you're not able to work it out, you can always ask a trusted adult for help. For example, you may be able to meet together with a counselor who can help you work out your differences.

The following activity can help you check if friendships are healthy.

HEALTHY FRIENDSHIPS CHECKLIST

To help determine if your friendships are healthy for you, think about whether you agree or disagree with the following statements.

- I have a friend I can count on, no matter what.
- My friends don't pressure me to do anything I don't want to do.
- My friends make me feel good about myself.
- I can laugh and be silly with my friends.
- My friends don't care what I look like.
- I can trust my friends with personal stuff.
- My friends and I have similar values.
- I feel like I can be myself around my friends.

If you agree with most of these statements, your friendships are pretty healthy! If you disagree with most of the statements, consider ways to branch out and form new friendships that may be healthier for you.

COMMUNICATING WITH FRIENDS

When communicating with your friends, there are healthy and unhealthy ways to express your feelings. Take a look at the lists below to see if you're communicating in healthy ways when you have a disagreement.

HEALTHY WAYS TO COMMUNICATE

Here are some healthy ways to communicate with a friend when you have a disagreement.

- Talk it out in person.
- Talk about it over the phone if you can't meet in person.
- Ask a counselor to meet with you both together. Express your feelings respectfully.
- Listen to your friend's side too.
- Apologize when you need to.
- Take responsibility for your own actions.
- Listen to each other's perspective, even if you don't agree.

UNHEALTHY WAYS TO COMMUNICATE

Here are some unhealthy ways to communicate with a friend when you have a disagreement.

- Ghosting: not responding to messages and/or blocking someone without communication. The only time this is okay is when you are feeling unsafe to talk to someone.
- Silent treatment: ignoring someone in person or online even after they've tried to talk to you.
- Expressing your feelings without listening to their side.
- Calling someone names—either to their face or behind their back.
- Refusing to take responsibility or apologize even when you did something wrong.
- Physical fighting.
- Posting mean stuff on social media about them.

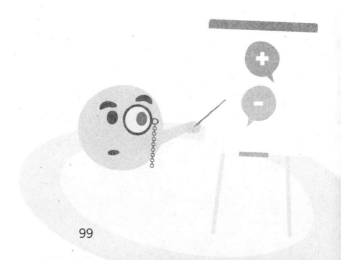

BULLYING AND CYBERBULLYING

In middle school, you might encounter bullying or cyberbullying, either for yourself or someone else. *Bullying* can be physical (hitting, pushing, stealing, etc.), verbal (name-calling, threatening, etc.), or social (spreading rumors, excluding someone, or humiliating someone). *Cyberbullying* happens either online or through texting and could include things like name-calling, posting photos without someone's consent, threatening to expose certain photos, sharing someone's personal information online, or creating fake accounts to harass someone.

Almost all states have laws regarding bullying, and schools are required to discipline students who do it. In fact, bullying can even have criminal consequences if the content is about someone's race, gender, sexual orientation, or other categories that would be considered discrimination. There can also be very serious consequences for bullying that involves sexual harassment or stalking. Bullying and cyberbullying, especially if it's ongoing and left unaddressed, can have serious consequences. Some girls who have experienced bullying end up feeling sad, depressed, anxious, or even suicidal. It's important to take this seriously and to report bullying to a trusted adult if it's happening to you or someone else. If you've reported bullying and it's still happening, report it again, and don't give up until it stops. Your parents, guardians, and adults at school have a responsibility to keep you safe, but they can't do that if they don't know that it's going on.

In addition to bullying and cyberbullying, girls in middle school often struggle with how to handle gossip. *Gossip* is when you talk about someone else behind their back, often about something personal. Gossip is usually negative, and sometimes untrue. For example, if you see a girl across the quad at lunch and you say to your friend, "Wow, I love her skirt!" that's not gossip. But if you see a girl across the quad at lunch and you say to your friend, "Hey, look, that's Jessica over there—did you hear that her boyfriend broke up with her? I heard she cheated on him," that's gossip! It can sometimes be tempting to want to share negative information about others, but ultimately it doesn't serve you or anyone else. Remember to treat others as you'd want to be treated, and if it's not your business, don't share it!

As you continue through middle school, try to keep your communication healthy and get help from a trusted adult if you experience or see bullying or cyberbullying. Let's take a look at Cassandra's experience when she experienced cyberbullying.

Cassandra is dealing with an argument in her friend group. A rumor about her got out of hand, and now she feels everyone hates her. She was on her phone at home when suddenly she got a DM from an unknown account. All it said was "go kill urself." Cassandra was shocked when she saw it. She had already been feeling depressed, and the message made her feel even worse. When her mom walked into her room, she found Cassandra in tears. "Honey, what's wrong?" she said. When Cassandra showed her mom the message, her mom talked to the principal the next day.

Cassandra did the right thing by telling her mom what was going on. No matter what kind of argument was happening in her friend group, Cassandra didn't deserve to be cyberbullied. Name-calling, references to suicide, threats, and sexually inappropriate messages should always be reported to a trusted adult.

What can you do if you've been bullied, or if you've seen it happen to someone else? First, resist the urge to bully back. It can be hard not to say mean things back to someone who is bullying you, but it's never a good idea and usually makes things worse. It's very important to report bullying of any kind, including cyberbullying, to a trusted adult. Sometimes people are scared to report bullying because they're worried that it will make the situation worse, people will find out they reported it and there will be retaliation, or nothing will happen. But because cyberbullying is harder for teachers to find out about unless they see the posts online and because it can get worse if nothing is done to stop it, it's extra important to bring it to an adult's attention. Many schools have options for anonymous reporting, where you can privately let school staff know about what's going on without having to share who you are. If there isn't an anonymous reporting option, know that school administrators are well trained in how to delicately handle these situations and preserve your privacy as much as possible. Even if there is a period of time where reporting the situation makes things more challenging, it's always worth it when the bullying stops. It's important to tell someone what's going on, even if you've been pressured not to say anything. Remember that your safety and well-being are always the top priority.

What if you have no idea who is doing the bullying since it's coming from an anonymous account? Even if you can't figure out who the bully is, you can still report it. Law enforcement has ways to track down an online bully. Take screenshots of the comments, pictures, or posts so that you can report them, and then block and report the account.

If bullying is affecting your mental health and causing feelings of anxiety or depression, make sure to talk to an adult for help. You don't have to go through this alone, and it can get better.

GETTING HELP WHEN SOMEONE IS BEING BULLIED

If you're concerned about bullying, whether for yourself or someone else, it's important to know how and who you can ask for help. The following are good options for who you can contact to report bullying:

- Your parent/guardian
- Your school counselor or school social worker
- Your school administrator or principal
- Your school's anonymous reporting system

REPORTING BULLYING

Next, let's think of ways you can get the conversation started about bullying. Grab your journal and write down some of your own ideas. To get you started, here are some ideas of what you can say to report bullying.

- "Mr. Simpson, do you have a minute? I think this kid Kyle in my class is getting bullied, and I want to report it."

- "Mom, I know you told me that you didn't want me to be messaging people online. Please don't be mad, but I wanted to tell you about some messages that I've been getting online because they kind of freaked me out."

- "Kacy, those girls at lunch were being really mean to you. I think we should go talk to a counselor together."

- "Mrs. Malone? Can I talk to you? This kid has been really bothering me, and I don't know what to do anymore. I'm really sick of it."

When you report bullying, you're keeping yourself and others safe. The sooner you report bullying, the easier it is to get it under control. By reporting bullying, you're creating a safer environment for you and your friends where you can focus on healthy and happy friendships.

By reflecting on your friendships, developing healthy communication skills, and understanding how to recognize and report bullying, you're building an awesome foundation for navigating friendships and relationships. These skills will also help you in the next chapter as you learn how to handle crushes and set boundaries that reflect your values.

CRUSHES, CATCHING FEELINGS, AND CONSENT

"I have a HUGE crush on this kid in my math class. Like seriously huge. I get so distracted...especially since my teacher changed the seating chart and now we sit right next to each other!"

—Nadine, age 12

You may find yourself getting crushes on people you meet at school. Girls in middle school may or may not have already started dating, but if they haven't, they've probably thought about what it will be like one day! It's a normal part of your development to start becoming attracted to certain people you meet and developing romantic feelings. Don't worry if you haven't experienced this—everyone develops at their own pace.

Getting a crush on someone or "catching feelings" can be a really exciting experience. It can feel exhilarating if someone you've had a crush on notices you, looks at you, talks to you, or even likes you back. When a crush is intense, you might find yourself distracted and thinking about this person throughout the day. You might find yourself feeling nervous or self-conscious around them. You might even find yourself looking them up on social media to see who they hang out with or learn more about them. Having a crush on someone could be something private that you keep to yourself, or it could be something that you want to tell all your friends about!

When it comes to crushes and friendships, things can sometimes get a little tricky. What happens if you and your best friend like the same person? Or if your crush likes your friend, but they don't like you? What happens if you get a crush on someone, but you find out they're already dating someone else? What if a friend has a crush on you, but you see them as just a friend? This chapter will help you to understand what a crush is and how to handle confusing scenarios.

Sometimes a crush is just a crush, and it doesn't go anywhere. You just like someone, feel attracted to someone, and that's it! Other times, a crush can turn into something more if you're interested in dating that person. What starts as a crush might turn into a talking stage as you get to know each other, and eventually you might want to start dating. When it comes to dating, your parents or guardians might have certain rules or expectations, and this chapter will help you to learn some solid communication skills to talk to them about dating.

As you go through middle school, it's important to start thinking about what your boundaries are and how to make them known. This can take a bit of practice! It's also important to learn more about what consent is and how to express it. These skills can help you feel more confident when you communicate.

GETTING A CRUSH

Getting a crush means that you start to develop romantic feelings for someone, and it feels different from a friendship. You might feel attracted to a boy or girl that you know, and you might daydream about them or wonder whether or not they feel the same way. You also might feel nervous or silly around them. Getting a crush on someone is really normal at your age. It's also okay if you haven't had a crush on anyone yet. There's no need to rush it! Let's look at what happened when Camila got a crush on Jake.

> *Camila and Adriana have been best friends since fourth grade. They started middle school together, and their friendship is stronger than ever. They have so much in common. They like the same TV shows, have the same fashion style, and even have a crush on the same guy, Jake. Every time they run into Jake, they start whispering about how cute he looks, try to get him to look at them, and then if he does, they burst into giggles. They jokingly fight over who gets to be partners with him in group projects in class. Everything was fine until Jake told Camila that he likes her.*

Adriana tried to act like everything was okay, but her feelings were hurt. Camila is so excited that Jake likes her back, but she doesn't want this to hurt her friendship. She's not sure what to do.

It can be tricky when you and a friend have a crush on the same person. While crushes can be really exciting, it can also be nerve-wracking to figure out what to do when things get complicated. Though Camila is excited that Jake likes her back, she's feeling conflicted about how to protect her friendship with Adriana. There's no right answer for what Camila should do. It's up to her to decide what is best for her and her friendship.

When you're in a challenging situation involving a crush, the best thing to do at first is to communicate clearly with everyone involved. Keeping secrets, hiding things, and pretending to feel one way when you actually feel another way won't help anyone. Camila could start by talking to Adriana about how she's feeling. She could let Adriana know how important their friendship is to her. Adriana will hopefully also be honest with Camila about how the situation is hurting her feelings and making her feel jealous. Depending on how the conversation goes and how they are feeling, Camila might decide not to pursue her crush on Jake for the sake of her friendship with Adriana. Or Adriana may decide that she is able to accept the situation and remain friends with Camila even if Camila spends time with Jake. No matter how they decide to handle it, it's important for both girls to communicate and make sure that their friendship is being considered.

REFLECTION ON CRUSHES

Grab a journal and consider the following questions. Write about any experiences you've had regarding the questions below and how you feel about them.

- Have you ever had a crush? What qualities did your crush have that made you like them?

- What was it like to have a crush on someone? How did the experience make you feel?

- What physical changes do you notice when you're near your crush? Does your heart start racing, do your hands get sweaty, or do your cheeks blush, for example?

- How would you handle a situation in which you and a friend liked the same person?

- How would you handle a situation in which someone tells you they have a crush on you, but you don't feel the same way? How could you communicate with them about how you're feeling in a way that still respects their feelings?

- Do you have an adult in your life that you're comfortable talking to about crushes and dating? What qualities do they have that makes them someone you can trust?

- Have you dealt with a tricky or confusing situation involving a crush? How did you handle it? Would you do anything differently?

Journaling can help you process your thoughts and understand how you're feeling. Once you've finished journaling about the questions above, see if you notice any sense of relaxation or clarity.

TO DATE OR NOT TO DATE?

So, what happens when you have a crush on someone, and then it turns out that they like you back!?! Maybe you start talking...maybe texting back and forth...maybe you follow each other on social media, if you have an account... and maybe at some point you start "dating"? But what does *dating* mean to you? Does your family have any rules about dating? Are you even allowed to date? These are important things to think about in middle school. Even if you haven't started dating yet or don't want to, it's a good idea to consider these types of questions, so that you're ready if and when the time comes.

Dating looks different for different people. Some girls might consider themselves to be dating someone if they know that they both like each other and they're spending a lot of time together at school. Maybe they both consider themselves to be dating if they're not talking to anyone else in a flirtatious way. Maybe they're allowed to hang out as a date in groups of friends at and outside of school. Maybe they're allowed to date one-on-one. Maybe they've held hands or kissed. What it means to date someone will depend on what you're comfortable with—and also what your parents or guardians are comfortable with. Let's take a look at what happened when Tiana asked her mom if she could go on a date.

Tiana is in seventh grade and Asaad is in eighth. They know each other because Asaad is the older brother of a girl on her dance team. Tiana has always thought Asaad was cute but was too shy to talk to him. A few weeks ago, he came up to her after dance practice and asked to follow her on social media. They've been messaging back and forth. Tiana is realizing she likes him a lot! The other day he asked her if she wanted to go get a burger with him on Friday after her dance practice. Tiana told him she needed to check with her mom first. She was nervous to bring it up to her mom because she had no idea whether or not her mom would let her go. They had never talked about that kind of stuff before. When she asked her mom, her mom kind of freaked out at first, immediately said no, and told her she was too young to date. Later, her mom came back and was calmer. They talked a bit more. They agreed that Tiana would be allowed to spend time with Asaad if her mom met him first, and if they hung out in a group with other kids their age. Tiana was thrilled that she'd be allowed to see him, and she messaged Asaad back to let him know.

This was a more complicated situation for Tiana and her mom because they had never talked about dating before. Tiana had no idea what her mom would be okay (or not okay) with, and her mom was unprepared for the conversation because she didn't yet realize that Tiana might be interested in dating. Thankfully, they were able to communicate and come to an agreement.

There's a wide variety of experiences that girls can go through when it comes to dating. Some girls won't date anyone in middle school, which is completely okay! Others may date informally, and still others might end up in a relationship that feels very serious. Girls develop at different rates, and there's no set timeline for when you might feel ready to date.

Dating will also depend on what your parents or guardians are okay with. Remember that many parents are nervous about the idea of their kids starting to date. Some parents might be okay with it, and others might be completely against it because of your age or other reasons. It's really important to try to have open and honest conversations with your parent if you're thinking about dating. This is tricky for your parents too—they might have a hard time at first with these kinds of conversations. Remember that if your parents have rules for you about dating, it's because they care about you and want to keep you safe.

Let's do an activity to help you learn how to talk to your parent or guardian about dating.

TALKING ABOUT DATING

It can be tough to figure out how to bring up the topic of dating to a parent or guardian. Here are some ideas for how you can get the conversation started. Try to choose a time when you're both calm and not distracted.

- "Hey, Mom, I was kind of wondering how old you think I should be to be able to start dating?"

- "Dad? Can I ask you something? This kid at school asked me to go to the movies with him on Friday. Can I go?"

- "Tía, there's this girl I've been talking to at school, and I think I kind of like her. Would it be okay for her to come over after school so you can meet her?"

- "Mom, how old were you when you started dating? What was your first date like?"

- "Dad, how come I'm not allowed to date? I want to understand the reasons why I can't."

- "Mom, don't freak out, okay? I just wanted to talk to you about this guy I met online. We started messaging each other. I kind of wanted to see what you think about him."

These are just some examples of how you can start to talk to your parent or guardian about crushes and dating. See what feels right for you!

Now, write some ways to start the conversation in your own words.

PERSONAL BOUNDARIES AND CONSENT

Boundaries are limits and guidelines that you can set for yourself, based on what you're comfortable with. Have you ever felt like someone got too close in your personal space? Like maybe someone was sitting too close to you on a bench or talking right up next to your face? That's an example of a way in which someone may have crossed a personal boundary for you. When it comes to our bodies and personal space, we all have personal boundaries. Yours might include, for instance, whether or not you like to be tickled or hugged.

When you make your boundaries known to other people, it helps them understand what you're comfortable with—and it helps them respect you too. When it comes to crushes, dating, and what you're physically comfortable with, it's important to consider what your personal limits might be and how to communicate them if you need to.

Consent means permission to do something. For example, if someone says, "Hey, can I sit with you at lunch?" and you say, "Sure!" you just gave consent (permission) for that person to sit with you. If someone texts you and says, "Hey, you're cute, can you send me a pic of you in a bikini?" and you say "nah" or decide to block the person who asked you, you did not give consent. Giving and getting consent is important. When two people are going to do anything physical together, whether holding hands, hugging, kissing, or something more, it's important that both people feel comfortable, their personal boundaries are respected, and they give consent. Let's take a look at what happened when Eve had an experience at school that she didn't consent to.

Eve was bending down and getting some books out of her locker when she felt someone slap her butt. She spun around quickly and saw a group of boys laughing and running past her. Eve turned bright red and tears welled up in her eyes. She felt angry and humiliated. Luckily, her friend Michelle saw what had happened, and she knew the kid, Chad, who did it. Michelle convinced Eve to go to the principal's office, and the two girls reported what had happened. The principal spoke with Chad, his parents were called, and he was suspended.

In this example, Eve's personal boundaries were violated and she did *not* consent to what happened. She did the right thing by reporting this to the principal, and Chad was disciplined for what he did. If you or a friend ever experience unwanted physical touch of any kind, it's very important to let a trusted adult know. There are rules in place to protect you, and you should never have to deal with something like this without support.

When it comes to consent, it's important to both give and get consent. For example, maybe you're the kind of girl who loves to hug everyone, but maybe you have a friend who's just not really much of a hugger. You could say, "Can I give you a hug?" and then your friend can decide yes or no. This is a way to ask for your friend's consent and her way to be able to give it to you. Consent can also be nonverbal. If you go to hug your friend and she freezes up, backs away, or tenses up, that's a sign that she's not giving consent to be hugged and would probably rather not be hugged. Pay attention to cues to notice what someone is comfortable (or not comfortable) with.

If you start dating, it's important to give and get consent for anything that you do together and respect each other's personal boundaries. These could include how often you talk to or see each other, how much time you spend with each other versus your family and friends, if you see each other alone or in groups, if you're comfortable holding hands or hugging, or if you're comfortable kissing or doing anything else. Before you start dating, it's important to think about what your boundaries will be. If you date, make note of any new boundaries that you discover.

The activity on the next page focuses on how you can identify your personal boundaries and how you can communicate consent.

BOUNDARIES AND CONSENT

When you know what your boundaries are, it makes it easier to communicate them to others. Take a few minutes to reflect or journal about the following questions:

- What are my personal boundaries?
- What am I comfortable or not comfortable with?

EXAMPLE: I'm not really a touchy-feely person. I don't mind when my mom hugs me, but I don't really hug my friends that much. I like my personal space too. I don't like it when my little sister climbs in my lap and starts pulling my hair and stuff. I just like my space and my privacy. I haven't started dating yet, so I don't really know what I'd be comfortable with yet. I guess once I go on a date eventually, I'd probably be okay with holding hands, but I think I'd probably want to know the person pretty well before I kiss them. I'm not sure about that part yet.

PRACTICE SETTING BOUNDARIES

Once you've identified some of your personal boundaries, practice out loud how you would assert them to someone. Here are some examples of how you can do that:

- There's a kid in your class who keeps doing things like high-fiving you, patting you on the back, and scooting his chair really close to yours. It's starting to get a little bit annoying. You could say: "I know you're just being funny, but I kind of need my personal space. Like...my personal space bubble, you know?"

- You and your crush have been talking nonstop sending messages back and forth for hours every day. But now it's getting in the way of your homework, and your mom is getting mad. You could say: "Hey, my mom is starting to get mad, and I really need to finish my homework. I don't want to get a bad grade in my class. Let's talk in a few hours, okay?"

- You're on your first date ever, and you really like this person. But you're nervous and you're not really sure that you want to kiss yet. As the moment starts to get closer when you're saying good-bye, you can say: "I really like you, but I'm just not sure that I'm ready to kiss you yet. Maybe another time?"

- You've been talking to someone that you met online who goes to another school. You're sending messages back and forth, and then they send you a shirtless selfie from their bathroom with the message "now your turn." This makes you uncomfortable so you could say: "Hey, I didn't ask you to send me that pic, and I'm not comfortable sending you one back." Then you could block that person. Also, talk to a trusted adult about what happened.

- You've been talking to your crush for a while now. You're hanging out by the handball courts after school, and you really want to kiss him. You're not totally sure if he feels the same way though, and you don't want to kiss him if he doesn't want to. You could say: "Hey...I like you. Is it okay if we kiss?"

These are some examples of how you can assert your personal boundaries and discuss consent. As you go through middle school, think about other scenarios that you might encounter and how you'd handle them. There's no exact right or wrong way to communicate about these things, but the most important thing is to communicate. You've got this!

FINDING THE "ME" IN SOCIAL MEDIA

"My mom got me a phone for my birthday after I begged her for months. It's so much fun laughing at memes and posting with my friends."

—Fiona, age 13

In middle school, you're at an age where if you don't have a phone yet, you're probably starting to want one and you're probably noticing more people with phones and on social media. Having a phone is a privilege and a big responsibility. It can be really fun and liberating to have a phone, and it can also come with some challenges. On the one hand, having a phone makes it so easy to chat with family and friends, let your parents or guardians know where you are, listen to music, and see funny reels, posts, and stories on social media. On the other hand, it can distract you from homework, contribute to challenging social situations (think: drama in the group chat), and pose a risk for cyberbullying and online safety concerns.

Whether you have a phone yet or not, it's important to think about healthy ways to communicate with others online, especially on social media, as well as setting some limits with your phone. You may also notice a big difference between girls your age in terms of their phone limits. Some parents or guardians won't let their daughter have a phone at all, some set strict parental controls on the phone, and some allow access to a phone but not social media. Some may ask that their daughter have their location turned on at all times to keep them safe. Others may let their daughter have a phone without any restrictions or limits at all. Try not to compare yourself to others and remember that your parents or guardians may set limits on phone usage for your own well-being and safety. Even if it can sometimes be annoying, this is part of their job as parents, and it's part of your job to show them you can be responsible enough to have a phone!

Figuring out your own comfort level with your phone and social media can take some time. This chapter will help you figure out how you fit into the world of social media and how to post and communicate in healthy, drama-free ways.

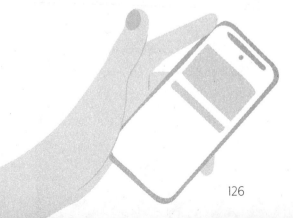

SOCIAL MEDIA

Social media refers to the different apps and online platforms that you can use to communicate with friends. Snapchat, TikTok, Instagram, and Discord are just some examples of popular social media apps that a lot of girls use to chat with friends. If you're allowed to access social media, it's important to think about your own personal limits and boundaries as well as any that your family might have for you. For example, which accounts are you following? What type of content are you posting? Is it making you feel good about yourself or is it stressing you out sometimes? Are you getting good sleep, or are you staying up too late watching reels? Let's take a look at Kaya's experience with social media.

Kaya's Instagram account is public, so anyone can see her posts. She has a lot of followers, and she loves tracking how many likes she gets. When she has something more personal to post, she posts it to her Close Friends group, so that only certain people can see it. Recently, she posted a pic of her hanging out with her guy friend/crush, Alex, to her Close Friends. But the next day at school, everyone was talking about it. She realized that someone had taken a screenshot of her post and was sending it to everyone—including Alex's girlfriend, Kim. Now the group chat is blowing up with accusations that Kaya is trying to get with Alex, and Kim sent her a DM threatening to fight her. Things are getting really intense, and Kaya feels totally overwhelmed.

Yikes, one little photo is turning into a big problem for Kaya. When Kaya posted to her Close Friends, she didn't think that someone would screenshot her post and it would end up getting sent to everyone, including Alex's girlfriend! Kaya feels upset that someone took a screenshot of her private post, embarrassed that her crush knows she posted it, and worried about the potential for a fight.

When you post on social media, always remember that what you post could potentially be seen by anyone, even people you don't intend to see it. Even messages and photos that delete after a certain period of time can still be screenshot, saved, or sent to others. It's a good idea to think carefully about what you post before you post it! (Imagine your parents or a teacher reading it. Would you still post it?)

It can be easy when you're scrolling through social media feeds to compare yourself to others. But remember that those posts are not real life! As mentioned in chapter 4, makeup, filters, and angles can drastically change how someone looks online. Using filters can even be part of the fun of creating pictures and posts! However, if you find yourself comparing yourself to others in a way that makes you feel bad about yourself, consider limiting your screen time.

Social media can be really fun, but it can almost be *too* fun and can be a major drain on your time if you let it. You might start by watching a couple of TikToks, and next thing you know, you've been doomscrolling for two hours! Middle school is full of exciting opportunities and new responsibilities. You'll have more homework compared to elementary school, as well as new commitments like sports practices, clubs, and school events, in addition to existing activities, like family events. If you spend a ton of time on social media, you won't have enough time for all the other fun activities. If your parents or guardians haven't already set limits on your screen time, consider checking your settings and putting limits on certain apps yourself.

For Kaya, her social media post created a lot of drama—and even the potential for an unsafe situation when Kim sent her a message threatening to fight her. If you're faced with anything unsafe on social media, it's important to let a trusted adult know right away. School counselors and administrators have a lot of experience handling these types of situations, and it's important for them to know what's going on in order to keep you safe. Kaya was feeling really overwhelmed by everything that happened, and talking to a trusted adult could help her get through it and prevent things from getting worse.

TO POST? OR NOT TO POST?

In this activity, take a few minutes to reflect on the following questions you can ask yourself before the next time you post.

- How does this post make me seem to other people?
- What's my goal with posting this?
- Would I be okay with anyone else seeing this post?
- Would I be upset if someone took a screenshot of this and showed it to someone else?
- Could this post make anyone else feel bad?
- Am I posting anything I might regret later?
- Does what I'm posting go along with my values?

If you're comfortable with the answers to those questions, go ahead and post! Enjoy seeing the likes, reading the positive comments, and connecting with your friends. But if you're posting *impulsively* (without thinking first), if you're reacting to something that made you upset, or if you're contributing to preexisting drama, then maybe pause and think twice about whether or not your post is a good idea. Remember that social media should enhance your social experiences, not make you or others feel bad, jealous, excluded, or insecure. If you're not sure whether to post something, spend a little more time thinking about it before you make your decision!

CYBERBULLYING

The friendships you'll make in middle school are going to bring a lot of laughs, fun memories, and good times. But what happens if things don't go as planned and arguments happen, feelings get hurt, someone feels excluded, or cyberbullying happens?

Some girls might think it's funny to post mean stuff about someone else online, or they might think the other person deserved it for something they did. But cyberbullying is never okay and should always be taken seriously. If you've been on the receiving end of cyberbullying or you've seen it happen to someone else, it always needs to be reported to an adult.

Let's take a look at Allie's experience with cyberbullying.

Allie is in seventh grade at Jefferson Middle School. Someone at her school started an account called Jefferson's Best Dressed—but really, the account was to post pics of students wearing ugly or embarrassing outfits. The account was created a couple of days ago, but it already has over 150 followers. Allie thought the account was pretty funny, to be honest. She didn't really think much about the account until a day or two later when she saw this girl Erika bending over to get something out of her backpack and her underwear was showing. Allie snapped a quick pic and submitted it to the account, where it got posted. A couple of days later, after school administrators tracked down the account holder,

Allie found herself in the principal's office having to talk about what happened. A mediation was held between her and Erika. Allie tried to explain that she didn't think the pic was a big deal since Erika's face wasn't in it. But Erika tearfully explained that everyone knew it was her, she was humiliated, and she was feeling too anxious to come to school. Allie felt really bad about what happened, apologized to Erika, and ended up getting suspended.

Allie never thought of herself as a mean or hurtful person, but her decision to make fun of someone else online had serious consequences. She figured that since Erika's face wasn't in the photo, that it wasn't really a big deal and wouldn't matter. She took the photo impulsively and didn't take the time to consider the impact that sharing it could have. Once everything unfolded, she ended up having a lot of regrets about what happened.

In chapter 6, you learned what to do if you're being bullied, but what if you realize that *you're* the one bullying others, like Allie? Take some time to reflect on the situation and ask yourself why you're engaging in mean behavior. Is it in line with your values? Are you feeling bad about something so you're acting out by trying to make someone else feel bad? Is it worth it? Remember that it's okay to make mistakes as you're growing up, but that it's important to learn from those mistakes too.

The following activity explores ways to respond to cyberbullying.

REPORTING CYBERBULLYING

Reporting bullying is necessary, but you may not be sure exactly how to report it or feel nervous about the consequences. Check out the examples of cyberbullying below, think about how you'd respond, and then check the possible responses.

SCENARIO: You're friends with a boy in your math class. You sit next to each other, and he always makes you laugh. Recently you saw a post where someone tagged him and was making fun of his weight and sexual orientation. You're really upset that someone would say such mean stuff about your friend.

POSSIBLE RESPONSE: You screenshot the post and show an administrator at your school so they can follow up.

SCENARIO: You posted a pic online, and a guy started flirting with you in the comments section. Your boyfriend got really mad and started posting all kinds of stuff about the guy on his stories, and everyone started piling on. Next thing you know, someone posted the guy's address, tagged everyone, and said "pull up."

POSSIBLE RESPONSE: Tell your boyfriend and others to take down the post. Report it to an adult as soon as possible, especially since the guy's address was posted, and his safety could be at risk.

SCENARIO: Girls in your class have been making fun of you online. They've been posting really mean stuff about you, and it just won't stop. You've reached a breaking point, but you're scared to tell anyone because you're worried that it will just make everything worse.

POSSIBLE RESPONSE: Take the plunge and tell an administrator anyway. Or file an anonymous report with your school's anonymous reporting system.

These are just a few scenarios to help you consider how you might respond to bullying. Each situation is unique, and if you're not sure the best way to handle it, remember to talk to a trusted adult for help.

SOCIAL MEDIA SAFETY

When you were a little kid, your parents or guardians probably talked to you about "stranger danger" and told you not to talk to people you don't know. They might have told you age-old lessons like: don't take candy from a stranger, don't open the front door for people you don't know, and don't get into creepy white vans, even if someone tells you there's a puppy inside. But what about when it comes to safety online? Is stranger danger something to be concerned about if you're safely behind your cell phone screen?

It's easy to feel like nothing bad can happen when you're just chatting online or posting pictures. And, while social media is usually safe and fun, it's important to be mindful of the risks.

Let's take a look at Jayda's experience below.

Jayda's in eighth grade, and she's been talking to this cute guy Ahsan who goes to another middle school in her town. They've never actually met in person. She knows some people who know him, and he hit her up a couple of weeks ago. They're both on the swim team for their schools, so they have that in common, and they've been talking every day. One day after practice, Ahsan sent her a pic on Snapchat, not wearing a shirt. He sent a kissy-face emoji with it, so she could tell he was being flirty. The pic deleted after a few seconds. Then he asked her to send him one back after practice because he thought she'd look cute in her bathing suit. She didn't really feel comfortable sending him a pic in her bathing suit, but she really liked him and the picture would delete after a few seconds anyway. She figured, maybe it wasn't a big deal? She's not sure what to do.

When you're messaging online or on social media, it's important to consider what you're comfortable with, what you're not comfortable with, and what might be a red flag for safety. For example, maybe you're comfortable having a social media account that's private, but you're not comfortable with it being public. Maybe you're comfortable sending pictures back and forth to your friends, but not to people you don't know. Maybe you turn your location on for your parents, but you don't share it with anyone else. Maybe you're okay with responding to strangers in a comments section, but not with talking to them in your DMs.

For Jayda, she was comfortable with messaging a cute guy she hadn't met in person, because some of her friends knew him and he went to a local middle school. But once he started asking her to send him a pic in her bathing suit, she started to get a little uncomfortable and wasn't sure what to do. On the one hand, she thought he was cute, and she wanted him to like her. But on the other hand, she wasn't totally sure she should send him the picture—even if it *was* going to delete after a few seconds.

When it comes to social media safety, the following guidelines are helpful to remember:

- Don't give out your private information, such as your address, school, full name, or birthday.
- Don't continue messaging someone who makes you uncomfortable in any way—block and report!
- Report any cyberbullying to an adult.
- Don't click on links that offer free stuff—it's probably a scam.
- Don't use your parents' credit card information for anything without checking with them first.
- If someone asks for suggestive or nude photos or sends some to you, block them and report it to an adult right away.
- Don't give out your passwords.
- Don't turn your location on for others to see. Use this only as a safety feature with your parents or guardians.
- If you encounter a situation online that you're not sure about, ask a trusted adult for help.

It's understandable that you'd feel like you can trust friends online that you make through gaming, social media, or other platforms. Or that Jayda would trust Ahsan since she knows he goes to school locally and is her age. But even when you trust someone, it's important to keep your safety in mind and follow the guidelines that will keep you safe. Sometimes it can be hard to know who to trust. If you're in doubt, talk to a trusted adult for help.

So, what can Jayda do in this situation? It sounds like she was uncomfortable when Ahsan asked her to send him a photo in her bathing suit. If something's making her uncomfortable, she should trust her gut. She shouldn't do anything that makes her uncomfortable. She could ignore his request or let him know that she's not comfortable sending it. If he is trustworthy and respects her, he won't ask again. If he continues to ask for more photos that she's uncomfortable sending, she can block him and talk to a trusted adult for more help.

SOCIAL MEDIA SAFETY

Reflect on the following scenarios and ask yourself how you would handle them if they happened to you. Then check out the possible responses.

SCENARIO: You love writing fan fiction, and you made friends with another girl online who loves the same fan fiction you do. She told you what city she lives in and what school she goes to, and she wants to know what school you go to. What do you do?

POSSIBLE RESPONSE: You could say, "Sorry, I never tell my online friends where I live or what school I go to." And then change the subject back to something you both enjoy.

SCENARIO: A guy who looks cute in his profile photo starts DM'ing you and asks your name. What do you do?

POSSIBLE RESPONSE: If you're not comfortable messaging someone you don't know, you could ignore the message or block him. If you'd like to message him, don't give him your full name. Try a nickname instead or tell him you can't tell him your name yet.

SCENARIO: Your Snapchat location is on and someone you don't know messages you and says they're at the mall too and that they want to meet up. What do you do?

POSSIBLE RESPONSE: Quickly turn off your location and block the person. Let whoever you're with know what's going on. This could be an unsafe situation.

SCENARIO: A guy from your school you've been talking to for a while starts to say sexual things to you that make you uncomfortable. What do you do?

POSSIBLE RESPONSE: If it's safe to do so, let him know that he's making you uncomfortable. Next, tell an adult at school about what's going on.

SCENARIO: A girl you thought was your friend starts making really mean comments on your most recent post. What do you do?

POSSIBLE RESPONSE: Talk to her in person about it. Let her know that she hurt your feelings and ask her why she did it.

When you take the time to think about potential scenarios, it can make it easier to handle them if they happen to you. If you're not sure how to handle the scenarios above, talk to a trusted adult for help!

RESPONDING TO PRESSURE

"This kid in my class got caught vaping last week. He ended up getting suspended, and his mom was SO mad."

—Claire, age 12

In middle school, you'll likely notice that not everyone is developing at the same rate. Some kids in your class might like to watch the same shows they did in elementary school, and others like watching shows designed for older kids or adults. Some kids have may have started dating, and others have zero interest in that. And, as you learned in chapter 4, some kids are going through puberty, and some haven't yet.

When you're in middle school, your brain is still developing and that, combined with changing hormones, can sometimes cause people to act without thinking. Not everyone makes impulsive choices, but you may notice some classmates taking risks, talking back to teachers, or doing things they regret. You may even notice yourself blurting something out that you didn't mean to say, or going along with what others are doing before you've had a chance to think about what's right for you. When classmates around you are making choices without thinking them through, and others are following suit, this can create situations where there's pressure to join in.

When you experience *peer pressure*, it means that one or more people around you are acting in a way that makes you feel like you should do what they're doing too. Sometimes peer pressure is verbal, when someone is talking to you and trying to convince you to do something or act a certain way. Sometimes it can be situational—you look around and everyone seems to be doing the same thing, and you feel a sense of pressure to join in too. It can even happen online, when you're looking at social media and feeling a sense of pressure to fit in. Peer pressure can be positive—like when all your friends are studying for a big test, so you decide to study too. But it can also be negative, like if everyone is making fun of someone. When you experience peer pressure, you may worry about what other people will think about you, whether you'll fit in, or whether people will like you.

It can take time to figure out how you want to respond to peer pressure. During middle school, you'll encounter situations where you'll be making decisions—positive and negative—as a result of peer pressure. You'll likely make choices that make you happier and ones that you regret. If that happens, remember, we're all human! Middle school is a time to learn, grow, and figure things out. When you're able to reflect on how to respond to these situations in a way that's aligned with your values (see chapter 2), you'll gain confidence in how to handle them.

FITTING IN SOCIALLY

During your tween years (and beyond), it's completely normal to want people to like you, wonder what people think of you, feel like people are staring at you, and worry about fitting in. This is a natural stage of development, and it happens to all of us. It's also a time when you're still forming your own values and identity and figuring out who you are and what your interests are. Not to mention, your values and interests will change over time. When the desire to fit in socially joins forces with the peer pressure to act a certain way, it can create some tricky situations. Let's take a look at what happened when Camila's friends wanted her to ditch class.

Camila had just started middle school and was making new friends. So far it was going really well! She met these two girls named Fabi and Ivy in her math class. Fabi and Ivy had known each other since elementary school, but they already liked Camila. A couple of weeks into the school year, they were scheduled to have their first big math test. None of them felt prepared—they'd been up late the night before sending messages in the group chat and hadn't really studied. Right before the test, they met up in the hallway. Fabi and Ivy told Camila they were going to ditch class since they weren't ready for the test and she should come too. Camila had never ditched class before, but she was worried about the test and didn't want to say no to Fabi and Ivy. She was worried about getting in trouble, but she decided to ditch anyway.

It's never easy to make decisions when you're faced with a situation in which you're feeling pressure. For Camila, it felt challenging to consider all the pieces of the puzzle. Ditching math class would let her put off taking the test and give her more time to study—if her teacher lets her take it later. Plus she wanted to fit in with her new friends Fabi and Ivy. But she also risked consequences from school (and possibly her parents) for ditching, such as getting suspended and receiving no credit for the test.

In middle school, there will be pressures to fit in socially in a variety of ways. You may feel a sense of pressure to hang out with a certain group, dress a certain way, listen to certain music, and try new things. During a time when you're figuring out who you are and what you like, there can also be pressures to define yourself based on others and what *they* like. It can be a little confusing! Remember that *you* get to decide your own interests, style, hobbies, and values. They're unique to you and no one else! That being said, it's okay to be inspired by your friends and to learn new ideas, tips, and shared interests with those around you. Friends who truly care about you and share your values will still be your friends even if your interests or choices are different from theirs.

It can also be tough not to let social media influence you, and you might find yourself comparing yourself to others you see online. You might be at home on a weekend, having fun with your family and relaxing. Next thing you know, you might see on someone's social media story that a group of people are hanging out at someone's house. This might cause you to feel bad that you're at home, wonder why you weren't invited, or question whether or not you're fitting in. In reality, there's no reason for you to feel bad or to second-guess yourself. Yet social media can sometimes have that effect.

Social media can also give the impression that others' lives are perfect even though we know they're not. It sometimes gives the impression that people are always going out, having fun, doing cool stuff, and looking amazing. In reality, we know that's not true! Remember that it's completely normal to have time at home, time with (and without) your friends , times where you're hanging out in PJs, and times where you're not laughing and smiling.

For Camila, the feeling of wanting her new friends to like her and her fear of the math test took over, and she gave in to the pressure to ditch class. This could have negative consequences for her including a lower grade in her math class. If you find yourself in a similar situation, try to slow down and think things through before deciding whether or not to give in to the pressure you're feeling.

REFLECTION ON PRESSURE

In this activity, take a few minutes to reflect on any times that you've felt pressured to be, look, or act a certain way or to do something you weren't sure was right for you. Grab a journal and answer the following questions.

- Have I been in a situation where I felt pressured?
- How did this situation make me feel?
- How did I handle it?
- Am I comfortable with the decision I made?
- What was the outcome of this situation?
- Was I okay with the outcome?

If you haven't experienced any significant peer pressure yet, you can use this time to reflect on how you might handle it if it comes up. You'll learn more skills on how to respond to peer pressure throughout this chapter. Remember that although it's normal at your age to want to fit in and to sometimes experience pressure, you always have the right to make decisions for yourself based on what feels right for you.

VAPING, DRINKING, AND DRUGS

In middle school, it's possible that you'll face a decision at some point about whether or not to smoke, vape, drink alcohol, or try another substance, such as marijuana (weed). *Vaping* refers to using an e-cigarette (vape pen) to smoke flavored chemicals, nicotine, or marijuana. While social media and TV sometimes make it seem like the majority of tweens and teens are trying substances, that's not actually true. The majority of middle schoolers aren't vaping, drinking, or using other substances. Let's look at some stats:

- The 2023 National Youth Tobacco Use Survey found that nearly 15 out of 100 (14.7 percent) of middle schoolers had tried a tobacco product at some point in their life. However, only about seven (6.6 percent) out of 100 had used a tobacco product in the past month (Birdsey et al. 202).

- In 2022, only 11 out of 100 (11 percent) of eighth graders reported ever having smoked weed (Miech et al. 2023).

- In 2022, nearly 9 out of 100 (8.7 percent) of students aged 12 to 13 reported that they had tried alcohol at some point in their life. However, only about 1 or 2 out of 100 (1.6 percent) had consumed alcohol in the past month (SAMHSA 2023).

Despite the low rates of substance use in middle school, it's important to understand the risks of smoking and drinking, so that you're better able to make an informed choice if you're faced with this decision. These are just some of the harmful effects.

- Smoking or vaping nicotine is super addictive and, among other harmful effects, negatively affects your lungs and brain, especially the parts that relate to learning, attention, and impulses.

- Smoking weed also has numerous harmful effects, including negatively affecting your lungs and brain, impacting your ability to learn and remember information. Additionally, kids who smoke weed are less likely to graduate from high school, and smoking weed as a tween or teen has been shown to have harmful effects on mental health, including depression and anxiety.

- Drinking alcohol at a young age has numerous harmful effects, including those that negatively affect the brain. It also increases risks associated with unwanted sexual activity, accidents, alcohol poisoning, and a higher chance of becoming addicted to alcohol later in life.

So, although some kids mistakenly think that using substances can help them improve their sleep or their mood, it's pretty clear that a lot of damage can be done by using substances—especially before your brain is done initially developing (in your 20s).

Let's take a look at what happened when Kailani had to decide whether or not to vape.

Kailani's parents moved over the summer after her mom lost her job. She was starting seventh grade at her new middle school. She didn't know anyone yet and was having a hard time making friends. She went into the bathroom during a passing period and saw a group of eighth-grade girls huddled together, vaping. When she walked in, the girls stopped and looked at her. Then one of them smiled at her, offered her the vape, and said, "Want a hit?" Kailani paused for a second and thought about how cool it was that an eighth grader was being nice to her. It was nice to be noticed, especially since she'd been having a hard time making friends. Then she thought about how mad her parents would be if she got caught, and how stressed her mom would be on top of everything else going on in their family. She decided it wasn't worth the risk, saying, "Nah, I'm good" as she headed into the bathroom stall.

When you're a little kid, it's easy to imagine that you'll never try drugs or alcohol when you get older. From a young age, we're taught that drugs and alcohol are bad and harmful. But as you get older, you might find yourself in situations where you're feeling tempted or pressured to try something new. Maybe it seems normal in your family or among your friends. Maybe you're going through a tough time and someone told you that it might help you feel better. Maybe you're having a hard time sleeping and someone told you that smoking weed will help (it actually messes up your sleep). Maybe you're hanging out with a group of friends, someone pulls out a bottle, and you feel pressured to drink since everyone else is. Or, like Kailani, maybe you're in a situation where you don't know anyone, and you think it might help you make friends.

When you're faced with decisions like this, it's helpful to reflect on your values. In chapter 2, you identified different values that are important to you—things like your education, family, athletics, culture, religion, health, and more. When you consider your values when making decisions, it can be easier to make the decision and can also help you be satisfied with the outcome. For Kailani, she valued her relationship with her parents, and she decided not to vape because she was worried about how mad they would be and also the stress it would cause for her mom.

The activity on the next page will help you consider how substance use could impact your values.

VALUES AND DECISION-MAKING

In chapter 2, you identified some of the values that are important to you. In chapter 3, you learned more about taking care of yourself. In the following examples, think about how those values relate to situations where you might be pressured to try smoking, drugs, or alcohol and the importance of taking care of yourself. Grab a journal and fill in the following prompts, keeping your own values in mind.

> **SCENARIO:** If someone offered me a hit off their vape, I would _____
> because I value _____.
>
> **EXAMPLE:** If someone offered me a hit off their vape, I would say no because I value my position as captain of the volleyball team, and I know that I would get kicked off the team if I got caught.

SCENARIO: If my older sister's friends came over and they all started drinking, I would _____ because I value _____.

SCENARIO: I really value _____ so that means I would/wouldn't _____.

SCENARIO: If a friend of mine started having a problem with drugs or alcohol, I would _____ because I value _____.

Can you think of any other scenarios that you've been through or might go through? How would you handle them?

RESPONDING TO PRESSURE

As you've seen so far in this chapter, the pressures of middle school aren't just about drugs or alcohol. There's pressure to fit in socially, pressure from your parents and guardians to be responsible, pressure from your teachers to succeed in school, and pressure from social media to look and act a certain way. So how can you respond to these pressures in a healthy way?

As we talked about earlier, peer pressure can be positive and motivate you to do healthy things, like a group of your peers studying for a test or your teammates practicing before the big game. When this happens, it's easy to respond to peer pressure and join in without any negative consequences. But when peer pressure is making you feel like you have to do something that you're not sure is right for you, it can be hard to figure out how to say no.

Let's take a look at Amalia's experience.

Amalia was hanging out with a group of friends the summer before eighth grade was about to start. There's a cool spot near her friend Justin's house where these big rocks overlook a lake. Everyone was hanging out, laughing, and having a good time. Pretty soon, Justin pushed his friend Sam off the rocks and into the lake as a joke, which was a pretty high drop. Sam was fine, and everyone was laughing. Pretty soon some other people started jumping in. Amalia didn't want to jump because she's scared of heights and wasn't sure how deep the lake was. But everyone was telling her to jump, and she wasn't sure what to do. Finally, she laughed a little nervously and said, "Nah, I have gymnastics tryouts next week, and I don't want anything to mess that up."

When you're deciding how to respond to peer pressure, sometimes you have to think on your feet. This can be hard to do when everyone is looking at you, saying things to you, or even laughing. It can be hard to know what to say or do in the moment. But don't worry, this kind of thing gets easier with practice, and this chapter will help you to consider different scenarios and how you could respond to them.

Amalia valued her safety, and she wasn't sure it was safe to jump off of high rocks into water—especially when she didn't know how deep it was. She also valued athletics and had a goal to make the gymnastics team. She didn't want to possibly get injured and risk her chances of making the team. But even though she valued her safety and athletics, it was still hard to come up with what to say to all her friends when she felt nervous.

Remember that your values and your goals are yours and yours alone. No one can tell you exactly how you should handle a situation—only you know what feels right for you. Trusted adults, family members, friends, teachers, and other people can guide you and offer you advice and helpful tips, but ultimately the choices you make are your own. You will sometimes make mistakes, and that's part of the learning process. Don't worry if you don't always know exactly how to handle a situation, or if you make a choice that you later regret. This is part of how you learn, grow, and evaluate your decisions.

Even though Amalia was nervous, she stood up for herself with her friends, and she didn't give in to the peer pressure to jump into the lake. She was able to think of a reason for why she didn't want to join in, and she expressed that to her friends.

The next activity explores ways you can respond to various situations where you feel pressured.

RESPONDING TO PEER PRESSURE

Take a look at the following scenarios and think about how you might react. Then check out the possible responses for examples of ways that you could use words to respond to the pressure.

SCENARIO: This guy at school rushes up to you and gives you his backpack and asks if you can hold it for him until after third period. He seems kind of nervous.

POSSIBLE RESPONSE: "Nah, I have to get to class, I'm late!" or "Why?" or "Nope, that looks heavy, I'm good!"

SCENARIO: A cute guy you've been messaging on social media sends you an inappropriate photo. It makes you uncomfortable, and he asks you to send him one back.

POSSIBLE RESPONSE: "I'm not cool with you sending me pics like that." Or "Why did you send me that? I'm not okay with sending you pics like that of myself." Or "Dude, I'm in middle school, wtf?" or "Blocked and reported!"

SCENARIO: Two of your closest friends ask you to ditch class with them. You really want to go with them, but you're almost failing the class.

POSSIBLE RESPONSE: "Ugh, guys, I wish I could, but I really have to get my grade up." Or "My mom will be so mad if I don't pass this class—I can't." Or "My dad says if I get caught ditching again I'll get grounded for a month—sorry."

SCENARIO: You're staying up late playing video games online with your friends. None of your friends have to get offline yet, but your mom is starting to get really mad that you haven't gone to bed even though she told you to. You're at a super important part of the game, and you really want to finish.

POSSIBLE RESPONSE: "Ugh, guys, sorry, I have to get off now" or "Alright, I gotta go, my mom's getting super mad." Or "Gotta wake up early for school—see you tomorrow!"

SCENARIO: A girl you just met at school offers you a sip from her water bottle at lunch. You take a sip and realize it has alcohol in it. She's giggling and you think it's pretty funny too. But it tasted *so* bad, and you're freaked out that you could get in trouble.

POSSIBLE RESPONSE: "OMG! Is that alcohol? You've gotta get rid of that, we could get in major trouble." Or "Ugh, that's so nasty, what is it?" or "Ew, ha ha, I'm not trying to get suspended."

SCENARIO: Two kids in your grade get in a fight at lunch. You whip out your phone and get a video of the fight. Your friend says, "You got that on video? You *have* to post it!" You quickly realize that you took the video impulsively and that you'll get in trouble if you post it.

POSSIBLE RESPONSE: "Nah, I better not" or "Ha ha, I can't, you know the principal would suspend me too for posting it."

Can you think of other scenarios that would make you feel pressured? What kinds of responses could you give to a friend or someone you know who's pressuring you? Grab your journal and write as many ideas as you can think of. Thinking about these kinds of responses ahead of time will help you to handle these scenarios if or when they come up in real life!

FIGURING OUT FAMILY

"Things have been hard since my parents split up. I go back and forth between my parents' houses all the time, and I keep forgetting my books at my dad's house. Then my mom gets mad that I don't have what I need to do my homework."

—Aniyah, age 13

Your parents, guardians, any siblings, and extended family have likely been some of your biggest supporters throughout your life. This will continue to be the case, but it might look a little bit different when you're in middle school. When you were a little kid, you probably wanted to play with your family members *all* the time. You needed a lot of attention from your parents or guardians. Maybe you looked up to older siblings and wanted to copy everything they did. Your evenings and weekends were probably spent with family, and most of your time was with family when you weren't in school.

In middle school, you'll likely want to spend less time with your family and more time with your friends or by yourself. You might want more privacy when you're at home. If you're going through puberty, changes in your hormones might sometimes make you feel more irritable, which could cause you to snap at family members when they annoy you (or maybe even for no reason!). These changes are a normal part of growing up, and it can take a little bit of time to figure out the new and changing ways that you interact with your family.

One way to make this process easier is to practice communicating openly with your family members. This can be tough to do! When you're having a bad day it might feel like no one in your family understands you. And your family members might sometimes say the wrong thing. But remember, parents and siblings aren't mind readers! They won't know how you're really feeling about something unless you tell them. It can feel a little awkward or embarrassing to open up to adults in your family, but this is one of the best ways to work through any problems that you're having.

Every family is unique and has its own strengths and challenges. It can sometimes be tempting to compare your family to your friends' families. For example, maybe you notice that your friends' parents are together, but yours are divorced. Or maybe your friend's mom lets her use social media, but yours doesn't. Or maybe a friend's family seems to have more money or takes cooler vacations. It's important to remember that each family is different, and no one's family is perfectly perfect all the time.

In fact, some families go through significant challenges. When that happens, it can create a lot of stress. Stress at home can have an impact at school as well. When challenges happen both at home and at school, your support system and healthy coping skills can help you through the tough times. (*Coping skills* are the ways that people deal with stress and challenges.) In this chapter, you'll learn more about how to rely on your family for support, how to communicate with them, and how to cope (at school and at home) if your family is going through a challenging time.

YOUR SUPPORT SYSTEM

For most of your life, your family members have probably been your biggest cheerleaders. Your parents or guardians took care of you when you were little, but now that looks a bit different since you're getting more independent. In middle school, you'll naturally find yourself wanting to involve yourself in more activities at school and with friends, and your friends will become a part of your support system too. This is a good thing! But it can be hard to balance the time spent with family versus friends. Let's look at the situation that Audre is in.

> *When Audre was born, there were some issues going on with her mom and dad, so her grandma has raised her since she was a baby. Her grandma has always loved her and looked out for her, and Audre has always been so close to her grandma. Now that Audre is in middle school, she wants to do things like go to the movies and school dances with friends. But her grandma doesn't want her to go out after dark and says that she's too young to*

be going to school dances—that she can wait until high school for that. Audre feels bad because even though she loves her grandma, she feels like her grandma is too strict, and Audre is getting frustrated.

It's normal and common at your age to want to spend more time with friends. It's also normal and common for your parents and caregivers to feel nervous about your increased independence. Just because you want to spend more time with your friends doesn't mean you don't still love your family. And just because your parents have rules and expectations that may upset you doesn't mean that they don't want you to be happy. It can be tricky to figure out how to navigate these kinds of situations, and there's often not a clear right answer for what to do.

As you decide how you want to spend your time and who you want to spend it with, you're building your support system. Your support system can be made up of family members, friends, teachers, and other trusted adults. For Audre, her grandma is part of her support system. Her grandma loves her and wants to keep her safe. Her friends are also part of her support system, and she has a lot of fun with them.

In the following activity, we'll look at who is part of your support system and their role in your life.

SUPPORT SYSTEM

In this activity, you'll be thinking of all the people who make up your support system. This could be some of your closest family and friends, but this could also include people in smaller supporting roles, like a lunch lady at school who always smiles at you. Not only will you be identifying people who make up your support system, but you'll also be thinking about the positive qualities that they have and how they support you.

Let's look at Audre's support system as an example:

- My grandma. She's always been there for me even when my parents couldn't be. She loves me a lot. Even when she's strict, I know it's because she's trying to keep me safe, and she doesn't want anything bad to happen to me. She cooks for me and makes sure that I have what I need.

- Tasha, my best friend. She's so funny and she makes me laugh all the time, even when I feel sad. I can trust her too—I can tell her anything.

- Mrs. S., my science teacher. She knows that I get super nervous about speaking aloud in front of the class, so she finds other ways to include me.

- Mrs. Cohen, one of the leaders at my temple. She helps me get my community service hours done, and she always asks how I'm doing.

Now, write about your own support system! Grab your journal and make a list of all the people in your life who support you and write what qualities they have that make them supportive. Try to come up with as many as you can, even people who aren't as close to you. Any time you feel alone or are looking for some help, you can look back on your list and remember the people you have in your life who are looking out for you.

COMMUNICATING WITH FAMILY

When you were a little kid, you probably told your parents and caregivers just about everything. When you scraped a knee, when your sibling made you mad, and when you were scared, you probably told a parent or guardian. But as you've gotten older, the amount that you communicate to your parents may be changing. You may keep things to yourself more than you did before. You also might turn to a friend for advice in addition to (or instead of) your parent. This is a normal part of growing up. But just because your communication preferences are changing doesn't mean you want to shut your family out entirely. It might just look a little different, that's all.

Middle school can be both fun and challenging. It's important to communicate with your family and your support system as you navigate those challenges. This doesn't mean that you have to tell your parents *everything* if you're not comfortable. But it means that you should try to communicate with them and other people from your support system when you can. In order for your support system members to help you, they have to know how you're feeling!

Let's look at Gina's experience.

> *Gina is in seventh grade. Her best friend, Eliana, recently told her that sometimes when her dad drinks too much, he hits her mom. Gina's really worried for Eliana and has been having a hard time focusing in class ever since she found out. She wants to tell her mom what's going on, but Gina's mom knows Eliana's dad.*

They go to the same church, and Gina's worried that her mom is going to freak out if she hears about what's been happening. Gina decides to go with Eliana to the school counselor to talk about what's going on. With Gina's permission, the counselor ends up calling her mom and filling her in on the situation and how it's affecting Gina. At first, Gina's mom was a little hurt that Gina didn't talk to her first, but she was proud of her for talking to a trusted adult.

If you have the type of relationship with your parents or guardians where you can tell them everything, that's great! But it can be hard sometimes to open up to them about what's going on in your life. You might be worried that they will freak out, you'll get in trouble, or they won't let you hang out with certain people or do certain things anymore if you tell them something. Try to remember that ultimately the reason why some parents and guardians have strong reactions to things is because they care about you, and they want you to be okay. If it feels too difficult to talk to a parent or guardian about something, remember that you have other trusted adults you can talk to. In Gina's example, she was able to have the school counselor help bridge the communication gap between her and her mom.

You may not tell your parents everything like you did when you were a little kid, but it's still important to keep the lines of communication open. When middle school is challenging, you'll need your cheerleaders and support system for help sometimes.

The following activity can help you improve your communication skills.

"I" STATEMENTS

When we communicate with others, especially about our feelings, we often start sentences with the word "you." For example, we might say things to our parents or siblings like "You wouldn't understand" or "You're so annoying!" or "You never let me..." When we start a sentence with "you," it typically makes the other person feel attacked, and they get defensive. This isn't very productive for communication.

Instead, try using "I" statements. The basic outline for an I statement is:

I feel _____ when

_____ because

_____.

"I" statements allow you to express your feelings more clearly, and the person you're talking to is less likely to feel attacked.

Let's look at some examples:

- **INSTEAD OF SAYING:** "You're so annoying" to your brother, you could say, "I feel so annoyed when the TV channel gets changed because I can't finish what I'm watching."

- **INSTEAD OF SAYING:** "You never let me hang out with my friends" to your mom, you could say, "I feel frustrated when my friends get to hang out together and I can't go because I worry they'll think I don't want to see them."

- **INSTEAD OF SAYING:** "You always make me start my homework right when I get home," you could say, "I feel tired and hungry when I get home from school, and I need a snack before I can get the energy to start my homework."

The next time you want to communicate clearly to your family, especially about how you feel about something, try using "I" statements! It takes a bit of practice to get it right.

Grab your journal and write a few of your own to get some practice.

COPING WITH CHALLENGES

No family is perfect, and, in fact, some families have some pretty serious challenges. Grief, loss, separation, divorce, money problems, addiction, health challenges, and abuse are a few examples of some serious challenges that some families go through. When things are tough at home, it can impact kids at school as well. For example, some middle schoolers might have a hard time focusing in class, staying motivated to do classwork and homework, and remembering to do things. They might also talk back to the teacher. Let's take a look at Fatima's experience when her parents were going through a divorce.

Fatima's parents are getting a divorce, and the process has been really hard. Her mom and dad are living in separate apartments now, and she and her sister go back and forth between them. Her parents keep fighting about custody and going back to court. Fatima is getting so tired of it. Her mom keeps complaining to her about her dad, her dad keeps complaining to her about her mom, and she feels totally stuck in the middle. She feels tired all the time, her grades are dropping, and her teachers keep getting mad at her for not paying attention in class. The only thing that helps her is art class. She loves drawing and painting, and she gets to zone out for a while. At home, she puts music on while she draws, and it helps to distract her from everything that's going on.

Every family has its own unique set of strengths and difficulties. And those difficulties can affect kids differently, even among siblings. Fatima felt tired and was having a hard time keeping her grades up in school. When you experience challenges, it's important to rely on your support system as well as use healthy coping skills. Coping skills can be either healthy or unhealthy. Unhealthy coping skills are things like using drugs or alcohol to deal with your feelings, engaging in self-harm, taking out your feelings unfairly on other people, or shutting down. Healthy coping skills are things like reaching out for support, exercising, making healthy lifestyle choices, listening to music, making art, or getting counseling.

If you're going through some family challenges that are affecting you at school, it can be helpful to let your teachers know what's going on (if you're comfortable doing so). When your teachers understand what you're going through, they will be better able to help you if you're having a hard time. If you don't want to tell them yourself, you could ask your parent or guardian to tell them. Or you could ask a school counselor to help.

You'll be able to get through some challenges on your own or with the help of your support network. But how do you know when you need more help, like from a professional? In situations involving safety issues like abuse, domestic violence, or addiction, it's important to let a trusted adult know right away so that they can make sure that you're safe. Involving the help of a trusted adult means that you and your family will get some necessary support. If you feel like you might be experiencing symptoms of depression (such as loss of interest in activities, problems with eating or sleeping, feeling persistently down, sad, hopeless, or suicidal) or anxiety (such as sleep issues, nervousness, stomach issues, panic attacks), it's time to let an adult know what's going on. School counselors, school social workers, your doctor, or mental health professionals can help get you on the path to feeling like yourself again.

HEALTHY COPING SKILLS

When you're going through a stressful time, it's important to be able to use healthy coping skills to help you deal with the challenges you're facing. Not every coping skill works for every person, so it's okay to mix and match. By trying out a variety of coping skills, you can find what works for you! For example, some girls love meditating and find it relaxing, but others find it boring. Some girls love journaling, but others prefer talking it out.

Examples of healthy coping skills include:

journaling	talking to a counselor	taking a bath
talking to friends	writing poetry	setting boundaries
drawing	playing an instrument	cleaning/organizing
listening to music	songwriting	talking to a trusted adult
meditating	exercising	crafting
petting a pet	reading a book	walking in nature

Those are just some examples—try to think of your own! For example, maybe you have a hobby you really enjoy, such as baking, or you like to get outdoors and go hiking or biking to clear your mind.

In the following activity, you'll think about how you've coped with a major challenge in your life.

EXPLORE A MAJOR CHALLENGE

Here's an opportunity to try out one of the healthy coping skills listed above: journaling. Grab your journal and answer the following questions:

- When was the last time you went through a major challenge—either in your family or otherwise?
- How did you cope with it? Did you cope in healthy or unhealthy ways?
- How did the experience make you feel?
- What did you learn from it?
- What coping skills might have helped you deal with the challenge in a different way?

By using healthy coping skills, like journaling, you'll be able to tackle the challenges that come your way. Once you get in the habit of using them, it gets easier and easier. Think of them as tools that you have in your toolbox, and you can use them any time you need.

FINAL WORDS: NOT JUST SURVIVING, BUT THRIVING

As you reach the end of this book, know that you've done something really powerful. You've taken the time to reflect on who you are, what your values are, and how you want to take care of yourself in middle school. You've challenged yourself to think about some big topics, and you've taken the time to practice new communication skills and healthy coping skills. You've also given yourself the opportunity to think about how you want your middle school experience to be—personally, academically, and socially. That's an empowering process—and it's something to be proud of!

On the first day of school, know that you're equipped with all the tools that you need in order to be successful. Whether it's figuring out what to wear, how to open your locker, or finding your classes, you've got this! Take each day as it comes, and know that you'll be okay. Even if you make mistakes or things go wrong, this is part of the process of learning and growing, and it's normal! You've got your support network of family, friends, and trusted adults by your side, and they'll be there to help you along the way.

As you explore all the exciting new opportunities that middle school brings, remember to rely on your values and strengths. You'll also be able to recognize what it means when you go through changes in your emotions, feelings, or moods, and how to communicate with your family if you're feeling frustrated or need some support. Use the healthy coping tools you've learned for taking care of yourself, communicating with others, and dealing with challenges, increased responsibilities, or pressured situations.

Get ready for all the fun you're going to be having socially with your friends too! Middle school is usually full of laughs, activities, and adventures. If any social challenges come up, such as bullying or peer pressure, know that you've got the skills to handle them. And if any issues come up that are too big to handle on your own, your support network is there for you when you need it.

Here's the inside scoop: it's not just about surviving middle school—it's about *thriving*. Thriving means that you'll be growing, learning, developing, succeeding, and flourishing. It's empowering to know that, while there may be some challenges or bumps in the road, you can handle whatever comes your way. By using the skills and tools that you've learned from this book, you're well on your way to an awesome middle school experience!

REFERENCES

Birdsey, J., M. Cornelius, A. Jamal, E. Park-Lee, M. R. Cooper, J. Wang, M. D. Sawdey, K. A. Cullen, and L. Neff. 2024. "Tobacco Product Use Among U.S. Middle and High School Students—National Youth Tobacco Survey, 2023." *Morbidity and Mortality Weekly Report* 72: 1173–1182.

Miech, R. A., L. D. Johnston, M. E. Patrick, P. M. O'Malley, J. G. Bachman, and J. E. Schulenberg. 2023. "National Survey Results on Drug Use, 1975–2022: Secondary School Students." *Monitoring the Future*. Ann Arbor, MI: Institute for Social Research, University of Michigan.

Substance Abuse and Mental Health Services Administration (SAMHSA). 2023. "National Survey on Drug Use and Health, 2021 and 2022. Table 2.9B—Alcohol, Binge Alcohol, and Heavy Alcohol Use in Past Month: Among People Aged 12 or Older; by Detailed Age Category, Percentages, 2021 and 2022." *SAMHSA*.

Geraldine O'Sullivan, LCSW, PPSC, is a licensed clinical social worker with a pupil personnel services credential in school social work and child welfare and attendance. She currently practices as a school social worker in San Diego County, CA, where she provides mental health counseling services and crisis intervention to teens using therapeutic modalities, including cognitive behavioral therapy (CBT), motivational interviewing, and solution-focused therapy. In 2022, she was awarded High School Social Worker of the Year for San Diego County. O'Sullivan is coauthor of *The Girl's Guide to Relationships, Sexuality, and Consent*. She is also known for her published research on the topic of eustress.

Foreword writer **Lucie Hemmen, PhD**, is a licensed clinical psychologist in private practice. For thirty years she has worked with teens, their parents, and their communities in programs designed to maximize health and well-being. She is author of *Parenting a Teen Girl*, *The Teen Girl's Survival Guide*, and *The Teen Girl's Anxiety Survival Guide*.

More Instant Help Books for Teens
An Imprint of New Harbinger Publications

THE GIRL'S GUIDE TO RELATIONSHIPS, SEXUALITY, AND CONSENT
Tools to Help Teens Stay Safe, Empowered, and Confident
978-1684039739 / US $19.95

JUST AS YOU ARE
A Teen's Guide to Self-Acceptance and Lasting Self-Esteem
978-1626255906 / US $17.95

THE ADHD WORKBOOK FOR TEEN GIRLS
Understand Your Neurodivergent Brain, Make the Most of Your Strengths, and Build Confidence to Thrive
978-1648482809 / US $19.95

THE TEEN GIRL'S SURVIVAL GUIDE
Ten Tips for Making Friends, Avoiding Drama, and Coping with Social Stress
978-1626253063 / US $17.95

FIND YOUR SELF-LOVE HERE
A Creative Journal to Help Teens Build Confidence and Embrace Who They Are
978-1648482922 / US $19.95

PUT YOUR WORRIES HERE
A Creative Journal for Teens with Anxiety
978-1684032143 / US $19.95

newharbingerpublications
1-800-748-6273 / newharbinger.com

(VISA, MC, AMEX / prices subject to change without notice)   Follow Us

Don't miss out on new books from New Harbinger.
Subscribe to our email list at **newharbinger.com/subscribe**